the
ingrafting

the conversion stories
of ten
hebrew-catholics

edited by
ronda chervin

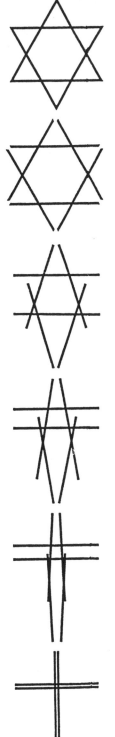

REMNANT OF ISRAEL
New Hope, KY 40052

Imprimatur: +Timothy J. Harrington
Bishop of Worcester

August 4, 1987

The *Imprimatur* is an official declaration that a book or pamphlet is considered to be free of doctrinal and moral error. It is not implied that those who have granted the *Imprimatur* necessarily agree with the contents, opinions or statements expressed.

Cover design by Basil J. Atwell, OSB

LIBRARY OF CONGRESS CATALOGING IN PUBLICATION DATA

The Ingrafting.

1. Converts, Catholic—Biography.   2. Converts from Judaism —Biography.   I. Chervin, Ronda.
BX4668.A1I54   1987   248.2'46'0922   [B]   87-9724
ISBN 0-932506-55-0

Published by   Remnant of Israel
New Hope, Kentucky 40052

CONTENTS

INTRODUCTION

"Let me put a further question then: is it possible God has rejected his people? Of course not...it will be much easier for them, the natural branches, to be grafted back on the tree they came from" (Romans 11).

* * *

I have never met a Catholic who was not fascinated by the story of how the grace of Jesus Christ led a Jewish person to become a Catholic.

Every time I give a lecture and mention in the introduction that I am a convert from a Jewish background, everyone hopes that I will get around to telling how it all happened. And, of course, I am just as interested in hearing about the conversions of others.

Such a small number are ingrafted each year, and yet we are a bridge to other Jews seeking to fathom the mystery of that Jew, Jesus, who sprung from the line of David and changed the nature of history.

The accounts contained in *The Ingrafting* have been chosen from among many such tales. They span a century, and include the story of a Chasid from the mountains of Hungary, born in 1899, as well as that of a young man from Los Angeles, baptized in 1984. Our converts come out of the richness of Jewish orthodoxy, the modernity of reformed Judaism, and the emptiness of contempory atheism.

Once Catholic, some of our narrators became monks, some priests, one a Sister, one a lay contemplative, others singles in the world, and some married with families.

Ingrafted onto the tree which is the Church of Christ, we have one thing in common: the passionate love for the One who came that all may be one. We hope that the reader may join us in praising God for the miracles of His grace.

Ronda Chervin

Utterly in Love

Utterly in Love

A Maryknoll Sister

(The Maryknoll Sisters are missioners in twenty-nine Third World countries on four continents. Our author was missioned to the Philippines and to the Central Pacific Islands. Presently, she is in mission at the Maryknoll Sisters' Center, Maryknoll, NY.)

*   *   *

"Play hopscotch!"

A chubby, freckle-faced Jewish girl dug into her pocket and found a small piece of chalk. Thick dark red braids fell over her shoulders as she bent to draw a diagram on the dusty pavement. Chalk was precious to Brooklyn children, so she used cracks in the cement for some of the lines. When she finished, Leah Feinman straightened up.

"You had the chalk, Leah, so you can have the first turn," the others conceded.

Leah tucked one foot under her and hopped into the first square, then into the next. Bits of trash—a torn-up bus transfer, an empty cigarette pack, some cigar butts, a flattened bottle cap—did not bother her. But she kicked a banana skin, stiff and black with age. It slid over a pavement crack to form a rude cross. Leah gasped and dropped her foot. The cross again. Always bobbing up when she least expected it.

"You're out! My turn next!" the children shouted, jostling for place.

Leah stooped over, gently picked up the banana peel and quite definitely placed it outside the diagram. Then she sat on the curb and thought about the cross.

But let Leah tell her own story:

*   *   *

I knew there was some mystery about the cross, something closely connected with me and my mother and my father and my four sisters, something about us all as Jews. I was conscious of it no matter where or how I saw it. Two pencils, two wooden beams, the stylized rays of a star, the moon seen through a window screen, the letter "T"—I saw the cross in each. The Madonna, too, fascinated me. Even as a child, I knew she was pure; this drew me to her.

Mama and papa were both orthodox Jews from Latvia. While mama lived, the feasts were full of joy and good things to eat and going to meet papa at the synagogue door in our brand-new dresses. The lighting of candles, the prayers, the two sets of dishes and utensils, the wine, the tasty little cakes, the gifts on special days all bound us together so closely. Yet even then I saw the cross form on the wall from shadows cast by the candles.

We had no boys, a big disappointment to papa. To make it up to him, I tried to be a boy as best I could. I hated dolls. I never had one any longer than a few hours at the most. Either I'd fall with it, or drop it, or give it to somebody else in a burst of generosity. Dolls were make-believe; I found plenty of real babies in the neighbors' houses.

Maybe that was why papa decided to send me to Hebrew school to learn Yiddish. Papa and mama rarely spoke it; when they did, we knew some nice surprise was going to happen. They wanted us to be good Americans, and nothing but English—albeit Brooklyn's—was spoken at home.

Yiddish school! I was delighted, especially because I would be doing something all by myself. Up to then, my three older sisters had blazed the trail and I followed meekly after. I used their books, wore their dresses, and had their teachers. I wasn't smart enough to know that Yiddish classes meant extra homework.

I registered late; most of the children already knew the alphabet. The first day I just listened and everyone was nice to me. The second day the teacher called on me. He used to walk up and down the aisle with a pointer in his hand. When he called on you, you were to answer fast. Somehow, I knew the part of the alphabet he asked me for. He beamed at me, but by then I didn't feel too happy about the whole idea of extra study. The third day was Friday and class was dismissed early so we could get home before sundown. My sister didn't know this, so she did not come early to get me.

I started out alone. It was three hours before a policeman picked me up and brought me home. Everyone was so glad to see me. Mama and my sisters hovered around and gave me everything I liked to eat. I remember so clearly cutting the crust off the loaf of rye bread and spreading it with mama's homemade cottage cheese. Papa came in soon. He had been looking for me, too. He went right out to buy chocolate bars with nuts, my favorite. Mama decided right then that I had had enough of Hebrew school; papa agreed. I loved them all so much; it was so good to be part of them! Thus ended my formal religious training as a Jewess. I was seven at the time.

Just about then, the Bassianos, an Italian family from Boston, moved into our duplex house. Mother and father and all seven children. Two of the girls, Angela and Rosita, were a bit older than I but didn't mind playing with me. We'd be right in the middle of a game, however, when they'd stop and say they had to go to confession or benediction or a novena. Sunday mornings, when I was ready to burst after our religious observance of Saturday, my friends had to go to Mass. They did their best to explain it to me, but all I gathered was that there was something holy about these activities. However, I did find out about the cross, Who died on it, why He died, and for whom He died. Angela and Rosita wore crosses around their necks, and sometimes they had medals with the Madonna on them. The purity of Our Lady appealed much to me. It seemed only right that she should be pure and clean from the very first second of her existence and that she should be a virgin when she gave birth to Jesus.

My sisters never played with the Bassianos. They had their own friends, much older than we were.

Thus the years passed. I would go off to meet papa at the synagogue and go home to the lovely and meaningful Friday and other feasts. Then, some evenings, after dishes were done, I'd be off with Angela and Rosita. Sometimes we would go to church; I would just look around and follow the words.

I must have learned the Hail Mary very early, because mama died when I was eight, and I remember saying it for her in church when she had been sick. One day she went away and, a week or so later, papa told us she was dead. Mama was brought home; papa let us look at her and then sent us out. I went walking with Angela and Rosita. A friend of theirs joined us.

"Leah's mother has just died," Angela said to explain why we were walking, not running around.

"Oh!" The girl was unsettled for a minute. Then she said, "Why aren't you crying? If my mother was dead, I'd cry."

I didn't answer but I thought, "She mustn't love God much not to trust Him." Mama was so good; everyone loved her. God must, too. I knew she was safe, but just to take care of any mishap, I said a Hail Mary every night and added, "Take care of mama and all of us and bring us to You. Amen."

Sarah, our oldest, was going to college. She organized the home. Each of us had a part of the house to care for with special emphasis on that part for Saturday. Sarah would tell us what to buy; we would place the order on the way to school and pick it up on the way home. She was home at three in the afternoon and we had a wonderful supper at six when papa got home. We still observed the dietary laws, but without mama, the feasts were no longer the same.

On Sundays, papa took us out on excursions. We went to the parks, to the museums where I saw more of my lovely Madonnas, to Staten Island on the ferry, on bus rides along Fifth Avenue, and to the spots in the city where Chinese, Negroes, Italians, and Indians concentrated.

Geography was my best subject, and when papa took us to Chinatown, I would lose myself in dreams of China or India—red pagodas, millions of people, clouds of incense, snake charmers, the sick, the lepers, the orphans—all waiting to be cared for, and I would help them. Just how I would do it, didn't bother me too much. I was just going, like the Apostles that Angela and Rosita told me about.

It was wonderful being with papa. I loved him so much. Sometimes we would just go along without saying anything but enjoying one another's company. We'd stop at a store to buy some crackers or cake, and then all of us would have tea and crackers when we got back home.

I finished grade school. My three older sisters had all taken the academic course in high school and gone on to teacher training college. I was expected to follow. By this time, I knew I wanted to be a Catholic, and I knew very well how much it would hurt papa. The best way to prepare for the break, I reasoned, would be to take a commercial course. Papa was surprised but not displeased. Money was scarce in depression years; my sisters were all teachers and yet could not find positions. So off I went to a different high school and took a commercial course. They were very much impressed when I came home and made all kinds of odd lines for long words. My glory was short-lived, however. One evening I got papa to dictate to me; he had to go so slowly that my sisters wrote it out in longhand and finished way ahead of me.

The years dragged through high school. I began to go to church more and more. Angela and Rosita and I went for long walks and talked about God. They opened to me the Rosary, the Stations of the Cross, the Gospels. They tried to get me interested in saints. I could not get enthusiastic about them, nice and holy though they might be, when there was the Blessed Sacrament and Our Lady. Her purity reached out to me and drew me close. I was happy and peaceful thinking and praying before the Blessed Sacrament. The Blessed Mother's statue was in the sanctuary, and I hesitated to venture inside the railing to light a candle. Instead, I went to a saint outside the railing, a rather sentimental nun-statue with roses dripping all over her. While lighting the candle, I made a point of telling that rosy nun the candle was not for her but for Our Lady.

It was real agony to watch the people go up to receive Holy Communion, and I could not. I knew it was the Body and Blood of Jesus Christ given for my healing and my life. I was hungry without it. How could some Catholics have this right and yet stay in the pews? Sometimes I had to get up and go out of church; I was afraid I'd go up with the people and receive Our Lord illegally.

It hurt me not to tell papa what I was going to do. But I knew I could not until I was baptized. He wouldn't understand and without the strength of Baptism, I could not withstand the pain of hurting him so.

Angela went over my weekly religion lessons with me. I believed everything; nothing troubled me. Even the Trinity, which baffles the theologians, caused me no distress. One evening the priest instructing me asked if I understood the Trinity. He smiled at my enthusiastic "Yes!" It seemed very clear to me; Jesus had revealed it, hadn't he?

I wanted to share all this joyful knowledge and picked on a school chum, redheaded Jewish Lettie. She listened and seemed to like it. One day during Lent, I walked her to church with me after school and showed her how to make the Stations of the Cross. She had no hat, but I snatched up a boy's cap left lying in a back pew and made her put it on. We went from station to station while I told her the story at each one.

The next morning Lettie was not at the bus station where we usually met. I saw her between classes but she was distant. After school I asked her to go to church again. Then she told me all. When she had informed her mother of yesterday's escapade, she was told to find another girl friend. After that, Lettie went to school on another bus.

Graduation came at the end of June. Three days later I was to be baptized. We all had dinner together just like every other Sunday dinner. I felt as though papa must know where I was going and I wanted to tell him. But I had no strength to tell him. Instead, I said something about going out. I loved papa and my sisters so very much.

It was June 28, 1936. A real hot summer day; the heat rose from the pavements and formed a mist as I crossed the street and looked back at the house. Papa was standing in the window. Angela was waiting at the corner. Her face fell when she saw me.

"Your dress," she said. "Why didn't you wear your white dress?"

I hadn't even given a thought to my clothes. I hurried back home.

"Why did you come back?" papa asked.

I gave a vague answer about wanting to wear out my graduation dress before the end of summer. I changed clothes, putting things on wrong and tangling my arms in sleeves. My knees were weak and it seemed an eternity before I was back at the corner with Angela. At the church, Father was waiting.

Eagerly, gladly, and full of expectation, I said I wanted the Faith and life everlasting. I received the Sign of the Cross—my glorious cross—upon my heart and my forehead. I renounced the devil and all his works and felt the chains fall from me. I assured Father that I believed in God the Father Almighty, in Jesus Christ His only Son, in the Holy Spirit, the Communion of Saints, the remission of sins, the resurrection of the body and life everlasting. Yes, I said, I willed to be baptized. I received the name of Mary, that of my lovely and pure Madonna.

With it, I got my white garment and my lighted candle for all men to see. I went forth in peace—that wonderful peace that goes beyond all knowledge. Now I really knew Him whom I loved and wanted to hold Him fast. After some time we left the church and started down the street, talking and laughing so hard we stepped right in front of a truck. We should have been killed, but, since He had promised to lift me up lest I be hurt, we were not scratched. I don't know how long we walked and talked, but we did get tired and went into a movie house. We kept on talking. The people were annoyed so we had to go out. Then we went to a cafeteria to talk some more. When we reached Angela's house, Rosita was there and we three talked some more. It must have been midnight when I turned the key in our door. No one was up. If anyone had been awake, I would have had to tell them I was a Catholic. It would have burst out of me.

The following Friday, I received First Communion. For some time I had been practicing with the round crackers we had at home. They seemed about the same size as the host. I almost choked trying to swallow them whole. Finally, I gave up. If God had brought me this far, he would see me through to First Holy Communion.

I went to a Holy Hour that same evening. When I came up the street, papa was sitting outside on the steps. I told him I was a Catholic. He just sat and I sat with him. He kept asking, "Why?" He felt I did not love him or my sisters any more. I was not loyal to mama and to all the Jews then being persecuted in Germany. If only he could realize how much more they were bound up with Christ and His sufferings! How much a part they were of the Gospels now, just as in the time of Christ. How I longed to suffer with them that some of Christ's sufferings would be filled up! But he could not understand why I had betrayed him so.

My sisters did not care so much, other than that it had hurt papa. Sarah was married by this time and I went to tell her. It made little difference to her, but she felt I was selfish in not considering papa's feelings. She asked me to stay for lunch and we had bacon and tomato sandwiches. I was shocked and surprised that she should have any kind of pork in the house. To this day, I dislike pork.

Before long, I knew it would be best to leave home. Every time I went to Mass, papa was upset. In the end, however, it was a can of sardines on Friday that brought things to a head. Usually, I ate out of the house on Fridays, but this night I got some sardines when the family had the usual chicken. Accidentally, I used the wrong dish for my fish. The whole evening was most unpleasant and we were all on edge. So I started looking for a room elsewhere. I had a secretarial job to keep me. Angela had entered Maryknoll by then. Rosita was married; she invited me to stay with her, but I thought it best not to.

The first lodging was a nice room with a private bath. However, I came home earlier than usual one afternoon and found the whole family coming in one by one to use the tub. "You're never home at this hour," they explained. I guess they did not get washed on Saturday and Sunday when I was home.

The next place lasted three hours. Rosita was helping me to unpack when an awful banging sounded on the door. Luckily the door was locked. It seemed the former occupant returned every so often when he was drunk and tried to get in.

The next day we found two houses with furnished rooms on a nice quiet street. After some ringing and knocking, a man came to the door, said there were no rooms, and slammed the door. Next door, a woman answered our ring and said, "No vacancies." That was that. We learned later that both houses had been closed by the police as red-light houses.

At last we found two rooms on the fourth floor of a house higher than any house around. The kitchen had windows on three sides. Two men lived on the same floor. They worked nights; the only time I saw them was on my way to Mass. All we ever said was, "Good morning." One day, when I paid my rent, my landlady returned five dollars to me. "I'm so happy to have someone so nice and quiet," she said. "You use so little gas and electricity, I'll reduce your rent five dollars." I record it here because this was probably the first time in history that such a thing occurred.

At this time, I met a group of Jewish converts and some Catholics who, to me at least, were intellectuals. We met quite often. I was amazed to hear about their "difficulties" before they could accept

Catholic doctrine. I had believed everything without the slightest doubt because God had said things were so. So they thought I was shy and treated me kindly and tolerantly.

They gave me books to read. Newman's *Apologia*; the life and writings of St. Teresa of Avila; the works of St. John of the Cross; Gertrude von le Fort's *Hymns to the Church*. Up to then my reading had been confined to my missal and the Bible, especially the New Testament and the Psalms. I was completely happy with them and my rosary.

I liked the *Hymns to the Church*. Newman was nice but he made no great impression on me. St. John of the Cross had me completely mixed up. St. Teresa made more sense—especially when she advised the nuns to eat more and drink a bit of wine. I had not had any wine since I had left home.

The saints were good and holy and what they wrote was surely right, but they just did not fit me at the time. My own conversion had been so simple. God had said, "Will you love me?" and I had said, "Yes, I will to love you." Then his grace came down to envelope me and lift me up. That was all there was to it. Even for the sake of these good people, I could not make anything more of it.

I started to examine myself more closely, to look for difficulties. There simply weren't any. I loved God for no other reason than that he is so very lovable. I knew papa and my sisters would have made wonderful Catholics. They were much more intelligent and could probably give excellent reasons for God's existence and his love and his ineffable choices. But the fact remained that he had fastened on me, and I did not think I should tell God he had made a mistake.

Some of my friends had difficulties about confession. I loved it. On my way home from work, I often walked over to St. Francis of Assisi Church on 31st Street and went to confession a couple of times a week. It was marvelous. All I could think of was grace and grace and more grace. I wanted to love God more and more.

Eventually I stopped seeing these friends. That is, all but Leon.

Leon was a Jewish convert, too. He had had many doubts, but he was so earnest in seeking God that God drew him very close to himself. Since baptism, Leon had abandoned himself completely to the loving hands of God. He was "the poor man of New York City," much as St. Francis was the poor man of Assisi.

We met just anyplace. We never planned a meeting, but I would be walking along the street or coming up from the subway, and Leon would be there. We would have a cup of coffee and a sandwich and we would talk about God. Rather, Leon talked and I listened. Many times, we sat for hours until the chairs would be piled up and the place ready to be closed. I still hear from Leon; he is just as dear and sweet and holy. His one ambition in life, if it be God's will, is to pass along to the next and more glorious life.

One Sunday afternoon I stayed home to listen to the radio broadcast of the Philharmonic Symphony Orchestra. I fortified myself with a bag of apples and picked up St. Therese's autobiography, *Story of a Soul.* Angela at Maryknoll had given it to me so I felt I really should read it. Several attempts to do so had gotten me no further than the first few pages. But this time I set myself to enjoy the broadcast and at least turn the pages from beginning to end. The whole thing took on new meaning. I forgot the broadcast and never touched the apples. The next thing I knew, it was seven-thirty and some terrific racket was coming over the radio. I snapped it off and went to church and took another look at the saint who had passed my candles along to the Blessed Mother for so many years. She no longer seemed sentimental. In reparation, I lit all the candles in front of her and hoped I would remember to pay for them.

So I fell in love with St. Therese. St. John, the Beloved, had preceded her. His Gospel had won me; his purity held me. He was an Apostle even though he stayed pretty close to home, not going around as much as St. Peter to Rome, St. Thomas to India, and St. Paul all over the place. I had never lost my desire to go to China or India. Now, too, I found out that St. Therese was patroness of the missions. My respect for her increased by leaps and bounds.

No definite future was in my hands; I was just happy being a Catholic, drinking deeply of all the Church had to offer. Angela at Maryknoll told me about Sisters on the missions. They were marvelous, of course, I thought, but it never occurred to me to be one.

One beautiful September evening in 1938, I came out of church and blessed myself. Right then, I knew I wanted to be a Sister, a Maryknoll Sister. I started home to write to Angela that I was coming up on Sunday. On the way, I passed a Chinese laundry and stopped at the door to beam at the three laundrymen working there. One finally asked me, "You have laundly tickee?"

"No," I told him. "I'm just looking." They must have thought me crazy and so I was—head over heels in love again!

Sunday found me up at Maryknoll with the biggest box of candy I could afford for Angela. I told her all about it and she called the Secretary General. And when I had told her, she gave me a large envelope full of forms to be filled out by doctor, dentist, laboratory technician, confessor, pastor, and, lastly, me. Rosita and I hopped around from one place to another distributing forms to be filled; then we called back to make sure they had been sent to Maryknoll.

I told Leon. He was delighted, and after we had been out of the Automat, we kept walking from one corner to another, talking about God until the wee hours of the morning.

I told papa, of course, and he just thought I was completely mad. My sisters did not react much more than to say that, again, I was being inconsiderate of papa. I never knew just exactly what he did, but he must have gone to the Bishop or written a letter to him. At any rate, Maryknoll told me to wait another year until I was twenty-one.

My trunk was already at Maryknoll. It was some comfort to know that it would stay there until I could catch up with it.

I had already given away all my clothes and did not see the sense of spending money on more clothes for an office job. In a factory, I could get along on two uniforms for the year. Once I was used to the clatter of the machines, the work was really quite peaceful. All I had to do was to keep a steady stream of soda pop caps flowing along a moving belt, and see that at the end they met up with some small circles of cork coming down a pipe. One cork was to hit each cap, dead center. It was prayerful work and I liked the people—Italians and Puerto Ricans, all of them supposed to be Catholic. I tried, but it was hard going trying to convince them that Miraculous Medal devotions Monday evening did not replace Sunday Mass.

December came round again. I set out for Maryknoll and really got there. I was going upstairs, clutching onto my coat and hat and hanging onto my suitcase, which the novice mistress was also trying to carry, when my belt buckle broke off and bounced down the terrazzo stairs making an awful racket. I was terribly embarrassed, standing there with my dress hanging loose and sloppy. But the novice mistress said, "It seems that your dress just can't wait to retire from service. The belt has made a complete break with the world." We laughed and kept on going.

*   *   *

So that's the whole of it. I fell in love. I fell completely, hopelessly, excitingly, gloriously, and stupendously in love. Even though it was years ago, the thought of it still sends chills up and down and all through me. As I write this, I am sitting in the Philippines, about five degrees above the equator, where chills are not to be ignored nor despised. God must be having a good laugh putting me and my Russian blood in the Philippines, five degrees north of dead zero. But, God willing, I'll have my own little laugh when I get into those pearly gates and sit down right in his lap, so to speak.

I'll remind him of the day his eyes fell upon a scrubby, chubby, freckle-faced, straight-haired Jewish girl playing on a hot city street in Brooklyn. And he said, "I love thee and have suffered much for thee. Will you love me in return? All that I have is thine. I will feed thee and clothe thee and bear thee up lest thou dash thy foot against a stone. I have prepared such delights for thee that eye has never seen nor ear heard of. Wilt thou love me?"

And I'll say, "You know everything, Lord. You know I love you. Lead me to those delights."

Originally published in *No Two Alike: Those Maryknoll Sisters!* by Dodd, Mead & Company (New York), 1965. Used with permission.

A Branch, Re-Ingrafted into the Olive Tree of Israel

Elias Friedman, O.C.D.

A Branch, Re-Ingrafted into the Olive Tree of Israel

Elias Friedman, O.C.D.

(*Fr. Elias Friedman is a Carmelite monk at Stella Maris, Mt. Carmel, in Haifa, Israel. The author of* Jewish Identity, *a pioneering book launching the International Association of Hebrew-Catholics, he is also responsible for* The Redemption of Israel, *published by Sheed and Ward, and innumerable studies in the areas of archaeology, poetry, and contemporary history, for which he has received many awards.*)

*   *   *

As I prepare to recount the events that took place in the innermost regions of my soul, I experience some embarrassment and trepidation. Encouraged by the permission of my Superior,[1] I will nevertheless attempt to give a sober and truthful account of the way which led me to the Catholic Church and to my religious vocation. I do so in the hope of spurring on others, if not to imitate me, at least to share my feelings of gratitude to Divine Providence, by the merciful disposition of which I was guided from the outer darkness into a wonderful light.

I shall begin by describing briefly my youth, as my conversion can only be properly understood against the background of my previous life.

The first twenty-two years of my life fall into two well-defined periods. The first period extends to my Bar Mitzvah when the Jewish boy, on reaching his thirteenth birthday, has to read a portion of the Law in the Synagogue, signifying that he is of age, ritually. The second period, one of agnosticism, lasted for nine years, until the moral crisis which brought me to a conviction of the existence of God and prepared me for the events that led to my baptism on August 5, 1943.

I was born in Cape Town (South Africa) on March 11, 1916 to Jewish parents of modest means. My father, who at that time was unemployed, had immigrated very young with his parents to South

Africa from Lithuania. In the same way, my mother arrived with her family in that far-off land from Poland.

Both grew up in their new homeland, for which reason Yiddish was little known and spoken in my immediate family circle. By hard work and thrift, my parents improved their financial position and were able to furnish their five children—of which I was the eldest—with a sound education.

At the age of six I began to attend the local school, and, sometime later, the Talmud Torah, where I acquired an elementary knowledge of the Hebrew language, attending afternoon classes three or four times a week.

Due to my mother's insistence, I attended divine services at the Synagogue on Friday evenings and Saturday mornings. For a time, I sang in the choir and remember experiencing a sentiment of piety and tranquility of mind during the singing. The major Jewish feast days were celebrated at home as well as in the Synagogue. In short, I grew up in an Orthodox Jewish family, though I cannot testify that a genuine religious life flourished there.

What I have described is all I acquired in my youth in the way of religious and moral preparation for life. Straight after my thirteenth birthday, I decided to stop practicing my religion until I could be more convinced of the religious tradition into which I had been born.

I should remark that the Jewish religion had not been presented to me as a belief to which one could give a rational consent, and though I recited the prescribed prayers, my heart was not involved. It may appear strange that a thirteen year old boy could adopt so skeptical an attitude to religion, but it is probable that it was because most boys of my age were doing the same.

The young child that I was launched himself on the seas of life with the lightest of baggage—which proved to be totally inadequate. Independent in my thoughts, I could be obstinate in presenting my views to others. In the period of agnosticism, I cannot recall ever denying outright the existence of God, but for want of instruction, I could not bring myself to any decision in the matter. In spite of recurring efforts to demonstrate the truth of tradition, my childhood resolution got lost in the sands, and I left the problem unsolved.

We lived in the Jewish quarter of the town. When I was fifteen, a neighbor introduced me to the Youth Zionist Movement. I began to take part in meetings, read books and brochures about the founder of Political Zionism (Theodore Herzl), and about the work of the Zionist Chalutzim (pioneers) in Palestine. In this way I made contact with "the Jewish problem."

I should say here that until then, I had not encountered Anti-Semitism, either at school or out of school. My new interest aroused in me a national sentiment; I realized that I was part of the Jewish people and shared their destiny.

With interest, I studied Jewish history, both old and new, as well as the condition of Jews in different parts of the world. I even took private lessons in Hebrew. The direction impressed on me by the Zionist Movement was to prove durable and to play a decisive role in my conversion.

I was, in fact, a Cultural Zionist, a follower of Ahad Ha'am.[2] I agreed that a Hebrew-speaking Cultural Center in Palestine would assure the future of Jewish cultural tradition, threatened with extermination by assimilation and the decline of religious faith. I called this the internal Jewish problem. (The external Jewish problem was the problem of Anti-Semitism.)

My young comrades elected me President of their group, but my period of office was not successful and at the end of the year I left the Movement, disappointed. The political views of my fellow-Zionists seemed to me to be confused. A National Home in Palestine would mean, quite evidently, that the Jewish people were no longer home-less, but that would be a mere verbal solution—if a solution at all. It did not enlighten me how it would necessarily put an end to Anti-Semitism. I also felt that it had no program for the entire man. My love for literature made me conscious of the limits of Zionist thought and made me see that many vital problems were neglected by the narrow ideology of the Movement. Wide-ranging and often heated discussions with young friends, who had travelled farther on the road to atheism than I, forced me to come to a decision in moral matters.

I was a medical student at the time, having entered college at the early age of sixteen or seventeen. (The choice of career was really that of my parents; I fell in with their wishes only because I was anxious to have a higher education.) At twenty-two, a severe crisis overcame me: I was attacked by a flood of skepticism, violent and incessant, which drove me from pillar to post until I found myself, finally, with my back to the wall. So powerful was the attack that one might have thought that it was more the work of a person than of an idea. Be that as it may, it condensed around the question: what and why to believe.

Driven into a corner, I could not bring myself to deny the objective nature of the distinction between Good and Evil. On this point I reacted with surprising sharpness. The outcome of the episode was a four-page letter which I addressed to a young friend with whom I shared my literary interests. In it I defended my position, basing myself on my own experience and that of mankind. I admitted my incapacity to advance any proof which would satisfy everybody for what I defended as a fundamental intuition. Nevertheless, my conviction was unshaken, and I acknowledged boldly the immediate consequence, valid at least for myself, which was none other than to accept the existence of God. If Good and Evil were realities—independent of the diversity of human opinions—then, in some mysterious way, the world was moral. And in no way could that be explained except by admitting that God exists. Further, I called on the order of the universe as an unquestionable demonstration in support of my position.

In this unexpected way, I escaped from the influence of the cultural milieu in which I had grown up, and from that of atheistic materialism on which the modern world was founded as on so much quicksand.

Unfortunately, the God whom I discovered remained for me the solution to a harassing intellectual problem and no more. My heart remained closed, and I could not bring myself to pray. Perhaps I had forgotten how to pray.

When World War II broke out, I was serving in a provincial hospital as intern. The next year, 1940, feeling that I had acquired sufficient practical training, I volunteered for service in the South African Medical Corps. After a brief period of training, I was posted at a large military hospital in the neighborhood of Cape Town. There, the entire development occurred which brought me to my baptism in 1943.

*　　*　　*

For a long time I had been growing conscious of a state of inner darkness and confusion, and contradictions in my conduct. It was as if some overwhelming force held me in its power. The crisis was deepened by failures which left me cast down and anguished, as if I were cut off from God. Overcome by my difficulties, I retired one afternoon to my room in the Officers' Quarters and stretched myself out on my narrow iron bed. It was then that grace touched me.

It is impossible for me to describe exactly what happened. It seemed to me that a thin ray of light from far and high penetrated my inner darkness. I felt as if God was reproaching me for withholding his admission to my heart in so rigid and obstinate a manner, even though for a long time I had conceded his existence. I was shattered by the justice of the complaint and felt compassion for God—if such a sentiment is possible.

When I rose, a new light shone in my eyes and I perceived that a way to salvation had been opened to me. From that moment I began to pray fervently, and embarked on an ardent search for God. I began to read the Old Testament and other kinds of religious literature. Grace gave me a deeper consciousness of the inner state of darkness and confusion from which I had suffered for so long. I remained shaken by the revelation. I did violence to myself to correct my faults and place my life on a new basis. The struggle went on for about a year, and so great was the dislocation that I fell ill with abdominal pains and was admitted to the hospital, signaling the onset of a chain of illnesses which was to last indefinitely.

After some months of treatment, I returned to my post in the military hospital. In the next few months, I took a decisive step in my spiritual itinerary: I discovered Jesus Christ.

Thanks to prayer, I had acquired a growing appreciation of the reality of God. Then the question arose in my mind: given the existence of God, whose goodness I had never questioned and in whose Providence I had every reason to believe, how could the Jewish problem be explained? The answer came in a shaft of light: Jesus Christ.

I immediately accepted the response as the best explanation, because it embraced the entire destiny of the Jews, without neglecting a single aspect, which was not the case with other pretended explanations.

The historical reality of the fate of Israel appeared to me so strong an argument for the divinity of Jesus Christ that all difficulties which my agnostic past and scientific formation could have raised against the possibility of miracles and prophecy, fell away. Therefore, Jesus was all he claimed to be: the Messiah, the Son of God.

The people of Israel had been exiled from its land to languish in a shocking dispersion for two thousand years, because it had not believed. The punishment fitted the crime.

I recall reflecting: if you believe in the divinity of Christ, why then, you are a Christian! In fact, I welcomed the thought—it was a source of happiness to me to think I was his follower, though I shared my secret with no one.

My newly found faith unlocked further fields for discovery. I began to read the New Testament, though I found it difficult to understand. I also began to read Christian theological literature.

I must have continued in this way for about a year, sympathizing with Christianity, without posing the question of baptism. What I wanted to know was how Jesus Christ could become the concrete solution to the Jewish problem. Evidently Jews would have to believe in him; my difficulty was to imagine what form of religious life they would adopt, given their acceptance as a collectivity. In posing the problem, I was influenced by my Zionist background.

Though I was not fully aware of it to begin with, I had raised the question of the Church. I realized that there were three possibilities open to a Christian Israel: it could be a part of an already existing Protestant denomination, a part of the Catholic Church, or an independent group with a Christian liturgy invented for the circumstance. In considering the three possibilities, the Catholic Church seemed to me to be the least disposed to make concessions to Jewish national sensibility in the religious sphere.

I soon reached the conclusion that it would be better for me to air the matter with someone who was more qualified than I to pronounce on the issue. The name of Dr. Martin Versfeld came to mind. He was a lecturer in Ethics at the University of Cape Town and a militant

Christian. Dr. Versfeld was of Calvinist origin, but rumor had it that he was a Catholic.

We met at his home in the "Gardens." He expressed himself openly about his religious views: for years he had been contemplating whether to become a Catholic, but a number of objections of an intellectual nature prevented him from taking the step. He feared, therefore, that he was not the right man to advise me on the particular question I had laid before him: in what church I should be baptized. (Since then, Dr. Versfeld, his wife, and children have entered the Catholic Church.[3])

My search went on. In the Officers' Quarters, there were several chaplains: Jewish, Protestant, and Catholic. One day, I entered the sitting-room and noticed what was evidently the Catholic chaplain, Fr. Charles Williams, engaged in reading a book. I entered into conversation with him, and felt at ease in his company by reason of his open and noble bearing. Fr. Williams, I learned, was an Englishman and had been an Anglican religious before his conversion to the Catholic Church. I asked him for a private conversation, and he conducted me to his room where I disclosed to him the state of my mind. It was the first time I had ever spoken to a Catholic priest.

I explained that, though I was a Jew, I had come to believe in the divinity of Jesus Christ. I then enlarged on my difficulty, asking him what religious structure a Jewish people which had embraced Christianity should adopt. Fr. Williams, I found, was sympathetic to the Jews, but he had to reply that, as he had never had to deal with such a question before, he would consult another priest about the problem. Would I return?

His consultant gave the following answer: the idea of a Uniate Hebrew Church, analogous to the oriental Uniate Churches, was unthinkable, for the reason that they were traditional and a Hebrew Uniate Church would be a novelty. I was disappointed.

Then, a word from Fr. Williams changed my sentiments. He observed that Israel's sin consisted in wanting to remain a national church, whereas Christ had given universal proportions to the Mosaic Revelation. The truth of his observation appeared manifest to me. Confiding my difficulty to the wisdom of Providence, I replied—to the astonishment of my interlocutor—that I was satisfied and would like to undergo instruction with him to prepare for my entry into the Catholic Church.

The reader will observe that my spiritual development was logical: from the existence of the moral order, I inferred the existence of God. Thereafter, I found my way to Christ, then to the Catholic Church, and, finally, my place in the Church. An invisible hand was unrolling step by step the parchment on which was inscribed my earthly destiny.

I awaited the day of my baptism with growing ardor, pressing my teacher to hasten. During my catechumenate, I was seized with a sentiment of sinfulness, such as I have never before and never since experienced. How I longed to be washed clean by the healing waters of the sacrament.

Finally, the desired day came. It was the afternoon of August 5, 1943, Feast of Our Lady of the Snows, when Fr. Williams and I left the camp for the nearby parish church of Witteboom. There my priestly friend administered the baptism. A Catholic doctor from Cape Town, himself a convert from Calvinism, was my godfather. I was conscious of the fact that something in me died and rose to a new life. Full of joy, I returned to my quarters.

The next day, I received Holy Communion from the hand of Fr. Williams in the nearby chapel of the Dominican Sisters. It is unnecessary to insist, after so many years of storm and stress, how much I appreciated the wonderful effects of this heavenly bread. My faith was strengthened; my cup of happiness overflowed. That my first communion took place on the Feast of the Transfiguration was something I ignored completely. I had too little knowledge of the liturgical calendar of the Catholic Church. Only years later did I realize how appropriate that day was, when Moses, founder of the People of Israel, and Elias, patron saint of the Carmelites, appeared with the transfigured Christ, conversing with him about his forthcoming Passion. Two weeks after my baptism, on the Feast of the Immaculate Heart of Mary, Bishop Hennemann administered to me the sacrament of confirmation.

Four months passed. One day, the director of the hospital called me to his office and advised me that I was to be posted to Robben Island, a small island situated six miles off the coast of the town. It had been included in the coastal defense of the town and its harbor. I received the impression that Providence stood behind the decision and so it turned out to be. I immediately left the town to take up my new duties. I spent two years on the island with leave to visit the mainland twice a month.

My duties at my new post left much free time at my disposal. I employed the opportunity to acquaint myself with Catholic literature, reading Maritain, Gilson, Sertillanges, and other Catholic authors with enthusiasm. At the request of Fr. Owen McCann, then editor of *The Southern Cross* and soon to become Archbishop of Cape Town,[4] I wrote an article on the Catholic approach to the Jewish problem, a concern for all minds on account of the Nazi persecution of the Jews. The theme of the article developed fast into a book, which I composed on Robben Island and which was published, eventually, by Sheed and Ward (London, 1947) under the title *The Redemption of Israel.*[5]

Here is not the place to present in detail the thesis I put forward. I remark only that the book contained the high point in my search for a solution to the Jewish problem which had occupied me since my entry into the Zionist Youth Movement at the age of fifteen. Reading the signs of the times in the light of prophecy, I reached the conclusion that Jewish history from the time of the French Revolution to the establishment of a Jewish National Home in Palestine announced the entry of Israel into the phase of salvation. God was preparing the homecoming of the people. The Christian era in the history of Israel was imminent.

It was and remains my conviction that the Apostolate of Zion could only be established on a national basis—that of an interpretation of Jewish history. The destiny of Israel was of significance to the world in general; would not their ingrafting be as a resurrection of the dead for the Gentile nations whose charity had grown cold? The drama of the Jews offered the key to a Catholic interpretation of the events of our time until the end of the world and the Second Coming of Christ.

When I terminated the manuscript, I asked myself what I proposed to do after the war. I thought of going overseas to specialize in some branch of medicine, a desire normal for a young doctor.

One Sunday morning after breakfast, I set off for the Camp Hospital in the usual way to make the rounds of the ward. I was seized by a strange unease which I was at a loss to explain. To calm the growing agitation, I set off for a walk along the lonely road which ran around the rocky coast of the island. It was a beautiful summer morning. I recall a flight of airplanes crossing the sky overhead.

Suddenly, I was brought to a standstill by an overwhelming impression. It was as if an invisible but clearly comprehended being was present before me, who ordered me with supreme authority to embrace the priesthood. Words cannot convey the force with which the command was issued to me. I heard no words spoken but the communication touched the deepest region of my soul. I confess that it was a painful, yes, unpleasant experience. What was there for me to do? One thing only: I had to bend and obey. The presence then disappeared, as if it had been waiting for my consent.

I set off again, slowly, on my way back to the Officers' Quarters and entered my room a totally changed man, fully deciding to leave South Africa once the war had ended and enter a religious order. No one knew of my project except the parish priest in whom I confided. When he asked me what order I intended entering, I answered that the Congregation of Our Lady of Zion seemed to correspond to my inclinations. Founded by Theodor and Alphonse Ratsibonne, both ingrafted Israelites, the Congregation directed its apostolate to the Jewish problem.

Two years were to pass before I left Cape Town for England in May 1946. In expectation of what lay before me, I took steps to prepare myself by studying French, as I knew that the motherhouse of the Congregation was in France, but Providence had designed my study for another purpose.

I left South Africa with the first available ship, which was a military transport full of British soldiers on their way back home from the Far East. No sooner had I made suitable arrangements for my lodging, than I entered into contact with the Fathers of Zion and told them of my interest in their Congregation. However, I first had to undergo an operation before taking any practical steps.

During my convalescence from the operation, I used to walk down from Kensington High Street where I lodged, to Brompton Oratory in South Kensington, in order to avail myself of its lending library. I read a great deal as I had been accustomed to do since my early days, my preference being for Church history and Scripture.

An unusual inner dryness plagued me at that time. My taste for reading diminished and seemed suddenly to have been paralyzed. The condition harassed me especially when I was on the point of entering the library.

I should remark that the books I preferred were to the left on entering; to the right were books on the Carmelite saints. My knowledge of the Carmelite Order was limited to what I had read in *The Story of a Soul* by St. Therese of Lisieux and a biography of Fr. Hermann Cohen, O.C.D. (a Jewish convert now being proposed for canonization). I actually experienced an aversion for the books on my right, as if they threatened to unsettle me in an indefinable way, but their presence obtruded itself on me more and more. An inner conflict ensued which I was unable to explain.

One day, I was literally held up, undecided, on the threshold of the library. Something pulled at my right elbow as if urging me to choose a book from the shelves to the right, about the Carmelites. "Very well," I said to myself, "for once it can't do any harm." I chose the smallest book to hand, as if to express how little interested I was in the Order. It turned out to be an anthology of excerpts chosen by an English Jesuit from the writings of St. John of the Cross.

I returned to my room in Kensington and read the book at one sitting. When I had finished I knew with unalterable certainty that God willed me to be a Carmelite, that he was leaving only one direction open to me along which I was to journey. I was granted an insight into the harmony between my own experience and the inner states which the Mystical Doctor of Carmel had so clearly described.

My Carmelite vocation took possession of me, body and soul, so completely as to exclude any other choice. I had been offered a light by which I perceived with absolute clarity that I had the soul of a Carmelite.

My certitude was stronger than my astonishment, which was considerable, as my knowledge of the Order and its spirituality was limited. As a precaution, I waited a few days to see if my enthusiasm might not wane. On the contrary, that was not the case; it pressed me with ever greater urgency. No choice was left but to renounce any hope of participation in the active apostolate to Israel and to enter Carmel.

I immediately informed the Superior of the Fathers of Zion of my sudden change of direction. With his recommendation, I went over to the Carmelite monastery in Kensington, rang the bell, and asked to be received. This took place in January, 1947. The London house of the Carmelites was only a ten minute walk from my lodgings, and yet I had not been moved to frequent it.

On entering the Carmelite monastery—a foundation of the Hebrew-Catholic Hermann Cohen—I was enveloped by the happy feeling that I was home at last. Strangely enough, I had visited the same Fathers a week or so before, to accompany another Hebrew-Catholic young man, who was an aspirant to the Order, and had left without experiencing any special attraction for the Carmelites. Now, Father Hilary listened with attention to my story and suggested that I return once a week so that he could study my vocation.

A fortnight later, I received a telephone call from the Prior: a Carmelite priest had arrived from Mount Carmel and wished to meet me. It was Father Edmund O'Callaghan, at the time Vicar Provincial of Mount Carmel. The Irish Fathers in Kensington had probably told him that a convert Jew would do better in Palestine than with them.

Father Edmund and I met on January 19, eve of the Feast of Our Lady of Zion, in the little parlor of the monastery. Having ascertained that my vocation was a firm one, he invited me to join him on Mount Carmel once I had been ordained. I accepted the invitation without hesitation. Providence, it seemed, wished to unite my first and second vocations. The next day I expressed my gratitude to Our Lady of Zion for her new favor.

In September that year I began my novitiate in Ireland, at the end of which I was sent to the South of France for studies in philosophy and theology. My ordination to the priesthood took place in the Metropolitan Cathedral of Avignon, next to the Palais des Papes, on June 29, 1953, Feast of Saints Peter and Paul.

I spent an additional year as a free student at the Catholic Faculties at Lyons, and then set off for Mount Carmel, via the Cape (to pay the family a visit), arriving at Mount Carmel on September 7, 1954.

Postscript

Once at Mount Carmel, my fundamental intention was firstly to make contact with the sources of Judaism and Zionism in the original languages. The second intention was to monitor the ideology of political Zionism.

In *The Redemption of Israel*, written in 1944 (published in 1947 by Sheed and Ward), I had affirmed with vehemence that political Zionism was incapable of solving the Jewish problem, because the problem was not a political but a transcendental religious one. Writing this postscript in 1984, I am able to say that my affirmation is now being echoed by many in the State of Israel.

In 1982, the South African Catholic Bishops' Conference, in Plenary Session, unanimously recommended to the Holy See my idea for a Community of Israelites in the Church. Their decision gave powerful support to the International Association of Catholic Israelites which I launched in 1979 and which is in the process of widening its bases with the collaboration of Msgr. Eugene Kevane, Dr. Ronda Chervin, and other devoted leaders.[6]

Notes

[1] This story was originally published in the *Southern Cross*, South Africa, and in *Die Wahrheit machte sie frei*, ed. Fr. Bruno Schafer (Trier: Paulinas Verlag, 1958).

[2] Ahad Ha'am (Asher Ginsberg, 1927) preached the establishment of a Hebrew-speaking Cultural Center in Palestine which he imagined would halt the spread of assimilation of Jews in the Diaspora.

[3] Martin Versfeld subsequently became Professor of Philosophy at the University of Cape Town and a distinguished writer in Afrikaans and English.

[4] Archbishop Owen McCann became in time the Cardinal Primate of the Republic of South Africa. He assisted Bishop Hennemann at my confirmation. Cardinal Owen McCann has been a consistent supporter of my apostolate.

[5] *The Redemption of Israel* was translated into Hebrew by Fr. Paul Bauchet, at that time a member of the Carmelite Order, and published anonymously under the title of

Ge'ulat Israel (Jerusalem, 1949). [Editor's note: The book can be found in English through library loan with the author listed as John Friedman. This name is explained by Fr. Elias as follows: "At baptism, I was stirred to beg Fr. Williams to give me the name of John, in memory of John the Baptist, who had announced to the people of Israel the approach of the Kingdom." Later, in the Carmelite Order, the name Elias was given to him. "These two names have always seemed to me to sum up my double vocation, to Zion and to Carmel."]

[6]For more information about this association, write to:

Charlotte Lowit
National Coordinator
International Hebrew Catholic Association
St. Michael's Church
424 West 34th Street
New York, NY 10001

Jewish Knight of Columbus

Arthur Klyber, C.SS.R.

Jewish Knight of Columbus

Rev. Arthur Klyber, C.SS.R.

(Father Klyber, C.SS.R., a member of the Congregation of the Most Holy Redeemer, has been a Priest-Religious now for fifty-five years. Though he is eighty-seven years of age, he is still vigorous enough to function as the Founder and Director of his organization, Remnant of Israel, Inc. The purpose of the Remnant of Israel is, candidly, to proclaim and write about Jesus of Nazareth as the Redeemer of the World, and as the greatest Jew who ever lived. Father Klyber also functions as chaplain of the St. Martin de Porres Third Order Dominican Community.)

* * *

"How did you become a Catholic?" This is a question asked of me from time to time ever since the day of my baptism February 8, 1920. It has struck me that this question is usually asked with the notion that a Jew's conversion has to be different from that of non-Jews. It must be something remarkable that would bring a Jew to Jesus.

Really, however, regardless of how many discussions about Jesus one has, or the number and kind of books read, every individual who has come to our Redeemer has done so only through a sheer gift of God.

People are only God's instruments in leading others to the Redeemer, but the *faith* in Him comes directly from God. No one else can give it. Every informed Catholic knows well that this Gift of God was paid for by Jesus the Redeemer on the cross. We are a purchased race. With this in mind, we can go ahead with the story of one Jew's way to Jesus the Messiah.

How it Came About

The Klybers and the Laschinskys emigrated from Berdichev, in

Russia, to the Ghetto of New York City around 1896 to escape further persecution by the Russians. My father, Samuel, married Julia Laschinsky; both sides of the family were strictly Jewish-orthodox. My parents brought a girl and three boys into the world before they both contracted tuberculosis and died of it, as did my two-year-old sister. We three boys were eventually committed to a Jewish orphanage at the ages of five and a half, six and a half, and seven and a half. But when I graduated from grade-school, my Aunt Ethel (my mother's sister) took me to live with her and her husband.

Aunt Ethel and her husband rarely talked to me about the Jewish religion, and, by the way, neither had any lessons on "Jewishness" been given to us in the orphanage. So, although I had been "Bar Mitzvahed" (something like Catholic Confirmation), the actual thought of God almost never entered my mind. My Bar Mitzvah ceremony took only about five minutes, and was all done in Hebrew, which I could read haltingly, but could not understand.

At that time, the only difference I knew between Jews and non-Jews was that, for some strange reason, Christian boys used to try to beat up Jewish boys.

I was without virtue, so-called, although I had picked up a lasting sense of honesty (don't steal, don't tell lies) through reading Horatio Alger's Boy-Books. These were based on the familiar proverb, "Honesty is the best policy." The accent, however, was not so much on honesty as it was on policy! Alger, if I recall correctly, never spoke of God in his books. He talked about the "rewards" of honesty in *this* world, such as success in business. I don't exactly regret his influence on me, since it was the only openly moral instruction I acquired in my early teens.

Despite three pleasant years and plenty of love in Aunt Ethel's truly religious home, I came away with religious practices but no deep religious knowledge or convictions. My older brother, Lawrence, remained faithfully Jewish, but my younger brother, Morris, married into a family of Baptists and adopted their religion.

Faith Nudges Me

On April 5, 1917, the eve of the war of the United States against

Germany, the young men of New York City were enlisting like crazy, and I was one of them. After a mere three weeks of training at the Naval Station, Rhode Island, I was detailed to the U.S. Ship *Fulton*, a submarine tender (mother ship) of the Sixth Submarine Flotilla at New London, Connecticut. I remained with the Flotilla for the full four years and four months of my naval service.

During the horrible flu epidemic of 1917, our ship was ordered to Charleston, South Carolina, where half of our crew was tranferred across the dock to another submarine tender, half of whose crew was seriously knocked out by the flu. That same night we sailed for the Mediterranean Sea, escorting three submarines, via Bermuda and the Azore Islands.

Aboard the *Fulton*, I had struck up what was to be a lasting friendship with a shipmate named Bob Anderson. Eleven days after sailing for the Mediterranean, while at anchor at Ponta del Gada in the Azores, there came a Sunday on which Bob invited me to go ashore with him to Mass. I went along dumbly, without any notion of what the Mass meant. The experience in that small crowded church left me bored and unmoved, especially since I had to stand up through it all. I came away from that experience just as much (or maybe just as little) a Jew as ever—but then, maybe God did something to me there which I didn't perceive.

Hound of Heaven

Back aboard ship that same day, we got the electrifying news of the Armistice, along with the further cheery word that our ship had been ordered back to the States, this time not to Charleston, but to the submarine base at San Pedro, California.

Some weeks after we had dropped anchor in the harbor at San Pedro (February 15, 1919), Bob invited me to his home in Los Angeles, about twenty-three miles inland. When I declined his kind invitation, he baited me by mentioning that their next-door neighbor had three lovely daughters. The bait did not hook me, but I finally hooked myself out of curiosity to meet Bob's family.

The visit with the Irish-born Mrs. Anderson (a widow) and her four sons—the youngest was sixteen—was pleasant. After supper, we went next-door where the dear Jewish mother introduced her daughters to me, and sat them down on a divan opposite me—for inspection maybe? Maybe you know that most Jewish mammas are candid about offering their daughters for marriage. However, I decided not to cultivate their acquaintance.

But with the Andersons it was different. I became a weekend nuisance at their home, and gradually the boys introduced me to their "exclusive" gang of Catholic young men and women. It turned out that this companionship was just what the doctor would have ordered for me. Of the twenty males and females in the group, I was the only non-Catholic. We all loved dancing, and we did a lot of it. We had frequent picnics, swims in the Pacific Ocean, mountain trips, and parties at their homes. This happy association lasted nearly two years.

Though none of them had ever asked me to become a Catholic, the example of their virtuous lives must have had a deep influence on me. I recall that my spiritual condition (if I can even call it that) at this time, was shabby, and I was heading for shipwreck on the rocks of loneliness despite their company. Still, as much as I can recall, I did not have any real "conscience" about the thing called sin—and I think that was because I didn't have any notable belief in God. It was at this time that the Holy Spirit chose to come actively into my confused young life.

Irish Delicacy

As I stood at the doorway of the Andersons' home one Sunday, waving goodbye as they left for Mass, one of them shouted, "Do you care to come along?" Strangely, without further thought, I hurried out to the car. In the church I was seated next to Bob. Now Bob was the usual "silent customer" as the saying goes. Neither in Ponta Del Gada at the Mass, nor now at Mass did he offer even one word of explanation of what was going on there at the altar. So, I bobbed up and down with Bob, or I stood up, or I knelt or sat; but none of those calisthenics strengthened whatever weak spiritual muscles I may have had. As at the Azores, so now, I left that Mass just the same as I was when I entered the church.

A couple of Sundays later I was out riding in the Anderson car with the family. Our conversation was about things in general, till suddenly out of the blue (or shall I say out of the green) the dear Mrs. Anderson asked me, "Arthur, why don't you become a Knight of Columbus?" Can you imagine any tactic so delicately (?) Irish as that approach— and so comical? Well, after a moment of speechlessness, I found my tongue and replied, "Aw, who ever heard of a Jewish Knight of Columbus?" And at that we both laughed, but when the laughter subsided, Mrs. Anderson pursued her attack by saying cutely, "Well, Arthur, you know it's not impossible."

So there, the message got to me, but it didn't convert me—at least not at the moment. The dear lady was brazenly asking me to become a Catholic. I merely chuckled, and then our conversation changed to other subjects.

God Scared Me

As I look back at that startling dialogue, I can't help regarding it as a near preparation for what happened to me that same evening aboard a Pacific Electric train to San Pedro. I sat down for a comfortable ride, but it pleased the Lord of Heaven not to let me relax. On that twenty-three mile ride, the moment of truth came to me without warning. In a clear sentence which I could not mistake or reject, but without the sound of a human voice, I heard: "Why don't you become a Catholic?" The Holy Spirit, it seems, was at that moment more blunt than the dear Mrs. Anderson had been in the car. I suppose the Holy Spirit was explaining that I *could* become a Knight of Columbus but that first I would have to become a Catholic.

Though the question on the train was attractive, it only scared me and started up a mental battle which was to last more than a week. My resistance, however, did not come from any Jewish doctrines, or from any unwelcome teaching of the Church since I did not know any such doctrines. My struggle came from a real fear of losing all my friends and relatives back home in New York, were I to become a Catholic. Somehow, I did know that such a loss of family could come about, though I don't know how I learned it. I knew only Jews who lived as Jews, and I had never even heard of any who had been ostracized for becoming Christians.

Back aboard ship that night I climbed into my hammock with a very troubled mind. Inside of me a Jew and a Catholic were having a wrestling match which continued, as I said, for about eight days. At that point, I figuratively put my foot down and decided: "I just can't do it, and I will not do it." With that decision, I seemed to capture some mental peace, but the next day the wrestling match began again. At some indefinite point the "Jew" in me began to yield, and I considered that, after all, maybe my family would not curse me. I also reflected that if they were to cast me out, I still had a nucleus of friends here in the West. That was the consideration which brought me final peace of mind, and helped me to risk becoming a Catholic.

A Navy Chaplain

At once I wrote a short explanatory letter to Mrs. Anderson (too embarrassed to visit her), asking her to tell me what to do for a start. She wrote immediately, expressed her joy at my decision, and suggested I see my Navy Chaplain. She also mentioned that she was mailing me two excellent books which were exceedingly popular at the time, both of which (she wrote) her deceased husband had used in his own conversion to Catholicism from Anglicanism. Those books were *The Faith of Our Fathers* by Cardinal Gibbons, and *Conway's Question-Box*. (I later learned that Father Conway had a Jewish mother.)

The next morning as I stood before the Chaplain and announced that I wanted to be a Catholic, he looked at me in astonishment and said, with a good-natured smile, "What? A Jew who wants to be a Catholic?!" He then handed me a small book to read and cautioned me against being in a hurry to join the Church. Believe it or not, the first half of that book was dedicated to arguments *against* the Church—it could have ripped out of me the still uninstructed Faith that I had. The second half of the book compensated to a degree for the dangerous developments in the first half. I returned the book with the remark, "Chaplain, I still want to be a Catholic."

He then arranged to give me a couple of instructions himself, and said he would turn me over to a Catholic Chief Petty Officer as my catechist. This fine shipmate gave me excellent instruction almost every day for a month and instilled into me some of his own deep faith.

One of the books that Chief Yeoman Kenny gave me to read made me see with much greater clarity who Jesus was: it was the then famous book *Quo Vadis* (Where are you going?), by a famous author named Sienkewicz whose books had been translated into many languages.

My mind and heart at this happy time were like the mind and heart of another Jew whom, years later, I had the pleasure of instructing in the Faith. That fine man said to me, "Father, now that I believe that Jesus Christ is God, just tell me what he wants me to do, and I'll do it."

During the eight or nine days of my struggle about the Faith, I had my usual walks and conversations with Bob Anderson, but neither of us said anything about the Catholic Faith. On one of those days he merely mentioned that the gang in Los Angeles was wondering why I hadn't come to see them lately and that they were afraid they had offended me in some way. I remember mumbling something about my not feeling up to visiting—I was going through my own secret battle. I think it was the morning after my first chat with the chaplain that I finally told Bob about my decision. All he remarked was, "I felt all along that you were thinking about that." He could read me well.

A Little Bit of Heaven

After a month of intensive instruction by Chief Yeoman Kenny, plus my own greedy reading of any good Catholic book I could get, I was baptized in the Church of Mary, Star of the Sea in San Pedro, with Bob as my godfather and Mrs. Anderson as my godmother. The unforgettable date was February 8, 1920; I was twenty years old.

The next day, as I stepped aboard my ship from the gangplank, a friendly shipmate named Reynolds almost knocked me over when he reached out his hand and said cheerily, "Congratulations, Art, I heard you were baptized."

My baptism was followed by an interior joy which defies description. I am not afraid to say that the joys of those early days in the Faith eclipsed, to a degree, even the joy of my Ordination. And, just as a note, I should mention that I *did* become a Knight of Columbus, as Mrs. Anderson had suggested, receiving all four degrees of the Knights within six months of my baptism.

In my long priestly life I have found that Jewish people who meet the Messiah and accept Him need such a lift at their baptism: most of them are punished severely by their loved ones for becoming Christians. Our families air their bitterness in words something like, "You are cursed by God for what you have done" or, "You are a traitor against your own People; you have betrayed the betrayed; you have gone over to the ranks of our enemies the Christians."

Nevertheless, a Jew who has accepted Jesus as Messiah has actually come to understand and love his People more than ever. Naturally and supernaturally he wishes for them with all his heart the saving faith with which God has blessed him.

"Completed" Jews (believers in Jesus), feel and know that in becoming followers of Jesus the Messiah they have only become what all faithful Jews expect to become when the Messiah for whom they wait and pray finally arrives. That is, we Jewish Catholics are deeply convinced that, in accepting Jesus as the Promised Messiah, we have become better Jews that ever.

Come, Lord, come into the hearts of all the Jews in the world, and even into the hearts of all people in the world!

You may order Fr. Klyber's very successful books for your own interest and as gifts for Jewish people by writing to Box 42, New Hope, KY 40052. These books include *He's a Jew* (about Jesus); *Queen of the Jews* (about Mary); and *Once a Jew* (a series of conversion stories).

Hope is Worth a Billion Dollars an Ounce

The Drogin Family
Back row, left to right: Elisabeth, Zoey, Ariel, Mark, Elasah, Paul holding Doriann Hope, John. *Front row:* Mercedes, Evamarie, Christopher, Peter.

Hope is Worth a Billion Dollars an Ounce

Mark and Elasah Drogin, T.O.P.

(Mark Drogin and his wife Elasah, both raised in Jewish families, were married in a Jewish Temple in 1969; five years later they both became Catholics. Now, with eight children of their own, they live in a Catholic lay community in New Hope, Kentucky. The community of sixty people, including children, is composed of families and single people. All the adults are members of the Third Order of St. Dominic and live a common life according to a Rule approved by the Dominican Order. The major apostolic work of the Community is their pro-life organization known as Catholics United for Life *[CUL] of which Elasah has been the President since its beginning in 1974. CUL is widely known for inventing and developing Sidewalk Counseling, the method of counseling mothers outside abortion centers as they go in for their scheduled abortions, offering them real alternatives, and assisting them in having their babies alive instead of going through with the abortions. Elasah, who had an abortion herself before she met her husband, is frequently invited to speak at pro-life and pro-family events about her own abortion, Sidewalk Counseling, or Planned Parenthood. She is the author of* Margaret Sanger: Father of Modern Society, *an exposé of the founder of Planned Parenthood—a book highly praised by all of its reviewers.*

The chaplain of their community is Fr. Arthur Klyber, C.SS.R., a Jewish convert to Catholicism whose story preceded this one. Mark and Elasah helped Fr. Klyber establish the Remnant of Israel and continue to work closely with him; Mark serves as President and Elasah as Vice-President.)

*   *   *

All of my grandparents, and Elasah's too, were among a great flood of Russian and Polish Jews who came to America at the beginning of the twentieth century, as did millions of others, with the hope of finding a better life. My parents were both born in Los Angeles where they lived all their lives. They had a strong Jewish identity and always taught my brothers and me to be proud of being Jewish. But I never knew what a Jew was because they denied all religion whatsoever— including the Jewish faith—claiming to be "cultural Jews" only.

Marx, Freud, and Einstein were considered three of the greatest Jews in all of history—a sort of trinity for modern, enlightened Jewish atheists; my parents were socialists and believed what they learned from Karl Marx: that religion was the opiate of the masses. God, church, and faith were meaningless concepts to be ignored in order to give all one's energy to the temporal world because there was no other reality. Human effort was seen as the supreme force in the universe.

My father was a dedicated humanitarian who taught me that the welfare of society was the highest good, and building the ideal community was man's greatest work. He was well known for his untiring struggle to improve the living conditions of all people. Because of him, as I grew up I always supported the most liberal position and progressive social change.

As a child, I seemed to be reasonably well adjusted and happy. I respected my parents, was generally obedient and honest, had friends, graduated from high school with honors, and entered a prestigious college with a scholarship. After making the Dean's honor list in the first semester, I suddenly found myself depressed and confused. At the time, there was a tremendous social upheaval tearing the country apart, and, even though I really didn't know what it was all about, I was swept into the torrent of young people who were rushing away from the "establishment" in search of "freedom." In a few months, I was alienated from the accepted values of American culture, and, by my twentieth birthday in 1965, I had flunked out of college and crashed head first in the "alternate society."

Even though my family was not rich, I lived those first twenty years in Southern California with every conceivable opportunity available to me. Then, suddenly it all seemed so futile, so incomplete, so empty— and wrong. There must be something else, I thought, something more, something meaningful, something worth committing one's life to. I was searching, but didn't know what for, or where or how to search.

Material progress in a Godless world with social values dictated by Planned Parenthood had been all I knew before the social revolution swept me into the so-called New Age of Peace and Love. I became one of the Flower Children and moved to Berkeley where I lived in someone's old garage when I wasn't hitchhiking up and down the California coast seeking, looking for visions, searching for hope, hoping for love, yearning to be free. It was easy for me to drop out of the "straight world" and tune in to the "counter culture," knowing somewhere in the back of my mind that my parents would always love me and take me back—and being old socialists from the '30s they really weren't so bad. I still wanted, however, to find some profound truth that was worth committing my life to. But my lack of knowledge and my desire for personal gratification led me instead to new depths of despair, loneliness, and hopelessness. My older brother told me he believed ours would be the last generation on earth because human beings were so corrupt they would soon destroy civilization. He was married and his wife soon became pregnant; I was baffled by what seemed to be an irreconcilable contradiction: society offered no hope, yet having children was a fundamental expression of hope.

Then I met someone who had real hope and could articulate it; my soul could not have been more receptive. "Let's build a society where everything is for the children," he said. "We will commit ourselves to helping each other raise our children and by working together we can build a community based on cooperation and friendship." What could be more hopeful than that! He was married and had two small children. I never knew why but I liked children—I was comfortable around them. Maybe it was because my mother had a baby when I was seven years old, and I always enjoyed having a younger brother. Philosophically, I was in complete agreement with the proposal to build a community where everything was for the children, and so I agreed.

There were others who agreed also; one of them was a young woman from a Jewish family in Ohio. A year later, we went back to her hometown and were married by her former Rabbi in the Jewish Temple she had attended as a child. Then we returned to California to raise a family in our new community where everything would be for the children.

It is remarkable how my wife and I arrived simultaneously at the same place spiritually, psychologically, and physically. She will now describe in her own words the road she traveled to reach this point.

*　　　*　　　*

I was born in 1946 of Jewish parents. I spent the first twenty years of my life living with them in a small mid-western town. Both of my parents also had come from large Russian immigrant families struggling for a better life in America. My mother would tell me stories about the cold-water walk-up flat they lived in, with newspapers on the floor to keep them warm; of the deep love she had for her mother and father; of the times she used to sneak into the Shul to listen to the prayers. My father's father had a small grocery from which he supported his five children. My father always expressed bitterness regarding his father's early death because he felt that he had worked himself to death. When my parents married they had real hope for a better life for themselves and their children as, I am sure, is true of most Americans of that generation from any background.

My family life was that of any American family which did not have the good forture of being strongly centered religiously; there is definitely a difference in families where religion is the first priority and where it is not. As a reformed Jew, I was taught pride in being a Jew, but not humility. The essence of my Confirmation textbook was that nothing can really be defined—not God, not sin. There is much I could have gotten out of my religious education and from attending the Friday night services, but I didn't. Somehow it all seemed meaningless to me.

I used to blame my parents for a lot of difficulties I had in my earlier years, but I have a different perspective now. Even though religion was not the first priority in my home, seeing my parents' good, loving marriage had a very positive effect on me.

I was the younger of two children—the thinking of the day was to have fewer children so you could give each one more, thus fulfilling the popular "quality vs. quantity" mentality so widespread today. I remember when I was about eight or nine years old, the thing I wanted most in the world wasn't another toy or a new bike, it was a new baby brother or sister. That was the only thing I can remember wanting as a child that I didn't get. The fruits of the "small family experiment" were responsible for the contradictory feelings I had that the universe revolved around me while at the same time I felt useless, bored, and empty because I didn't think I was needed by anyone. This set me up for nightmarish teenage and young adult years.

I had gathered from different sources some slight sense of idealism. Some of it came from the civil rights movement—I had a girlish fantasy about going out and living temporarily in one of the tenements owned by my father and writing a book about what it was like to be poor and discriminated against. I talked to my mother about wanting to be a "non-conformist" and I recall she said there was no such thing because I would always be conforming to something, whether it was beads and long hair or something else.

During the middle of the social upheaval, I went to California and was bewildered by everything I saw. In Golden Gate Park, for the first time in my life, I saw a woman breast-feeding her baby. Only then did it dawn on me what a woman's breasts were for—I was twenty-two years old.

A few months later, I was pregnant and went to Mexico to abort my baby—with no thought of idealism, with no thought of helping someone who was helpless, with no memory of the woman nursing her baby in the park. It was the end of a rapidly played out experiment for me. I saw nothing left in myself worth hanging on to. I thought I had tried all that life had to offer and did not want to play it over again. Any hopes or dreams I had seemed to have died with my aborted baby. I wasn't sure how I would go on or how much longer I even wanted to live.

By the grace of God, it was at this point in my life that I met a married couple who really loved each other. They were seekers looking for truth, and they had hope. There was something different about them: they were kind and generous and loving. They took me into their house when I was desperate—and they had two small children.

*   *   *

That is my wife's story about her abortion and how she began to realize the devastation that resulted from it. In retrospect, seventeen years later, we can see that it was clearly the grace of God that brought Elasah and me to that place in northern California late in 1968. The death of the hippies was proclaimed in San Francisco, yet we were still hippies with no understanding. No understanding, that is, until we met this couple who believed they could build a better world for their children. It was the same American dream that all of our parents had, the dream that had died in the '60s.

Suddenly, there was the vision we had been seeking, a reason for living, and our new friends were able to articulate the reason for their hope: "Universal truth exists. There is only One Reality and it contains no contradiction." Elasah and I had been drowning in relativism; trying to hold onto "nothing" was killing us. It was such a relief to meet someone who believed that we could agree on objective truth.

Both of us saw an enthusiasm we had never known before: our new friends believed that by seeking together—each person communicating his own point of view—we could perceive the true nature of reality through a process of "triangulation." By communicating with one another honestly, we could agree on our perception of reality in order to build the ideal society, a society built on hope in the future where everything would be for the children, everything would be for the future of humanity. We made this simple profession to each other: To stay together for life, always tell the truth, seek the true nature of reality, and help raise the children.

Our first dogma, our first article of faith, was that we really could discover the truth and determine the nature of reality accurately enough to build the best of all possible worlds. We would build unity through community and become of one heart and one mind so that everything we did would have maximum efficiency. "Two can do more than twice as much as one," we would say, thinking it was an original principle of economics. Now, of course, it seems it was only our materialistic way of practicing Christ's counsel, "Where two or three are gathered in my name...." The fact is, we were gathered in the Name of Truth and we didn't know what that name was. We were trying to discover the Real Natural Law. Whatever nature was, we were going to rediscover where it was and get back to it; rediscovering, somehow, the Garden of Eden, where we imagined we could in some way put Adam and Eve's mistake right.

"Let's do it," we said, and moved up into the mountains. We began to put our theories into practice, hoping to discover the secret of the universe through our unity. We were Americans educated according to the official motto of the American educational system: "Learn by doing." And the only way to learn by doing, we found—the only way to work out our own salvation with fear and trembling, to discover truth in nature—was to make a firm life and death commitment and stick to it.

Learning by doing, we learned things which could be learned in no other way. Mostly, we learned that we were wrong about mostly everything, but the premise of our hippie faith remained our guiding light: to keep on keeping on and never lose hope. We knew we would have to suffer, and we agreed to make whatever sacrifices would be necessary in order to create the best possible environment for our children.

We became country hippies looking for truth and a natural high (our first rule being "no drugs"), somehow seeing the innate goodness in the material world. The popular belief at the time was that Jesus Christ and Buddha were both enlightened men—two of many great holy people who had discovered the secret. We had believed it too, until someone asked, "What is the difference between Jesus Christ and Buddha?" We thought about it for weeks, we studied the sacred writings, we argued, we meditated, we were perplexed... and then the light broke through. We discovered that there is all the difference in the world between Jesus Christ and Buddha.

Buddha denies suffering, teaches one to avoid suffering, to ignore it. We found that suffering had no meaning according to eastern religions, for, to them, suffering, like all human experience, is an illusion; reality is an illusion. Jesus Christ, on the other hand, showed us that human experience has meaning. He was the only person who ever gave meaning to suffering: He came into the world to suffer. He taught us that suffering for each other is good, and that, by suffering on behalf of another person, we embrace the true nature of our humanity. Only then can we find Reality: God. I think the day we realized this was the day we became true Christians.

By this time Elasah and I were married and had our first baby, a girl. We named her Kama Zoe because it means "Desire Life." Two years after being married by a Rabbi in a Jewish Temple, we were now both Christians, professing that Jesus is the Promised Messiah who came to save us from our sins.

Time and again, I confessed my selfishness in one form or another and renewed my commitment, only to fall again into my old habits. There was a small weak voice of truth inside me saying that there was a God who taught us to love one another, but we would have to suffer the pain of overcoming our selfishness. Over and over again, for years, I tried to silence that voice but never succeeded—I always knew I would have to suffer and make sacrifices in order to love people.

My wife was experiencing the same painful process of repeatedly dying and being reborn; she admitted she could no longer deny that Jesus Christ was the Son of God, and God Himself. "I didn't really believe it," she said, "until I read Isaiah, Chapter 53. This was the Old Testament, the part of the Bible I felt, as a Jew, more confident in believing."

Both of us, actually, were spoiled brats who never had to suffer or put ourselves out for someone else to the point of sacrificing our own comfort in any way. We read over and over again that Jesus said "Love your neighbor as yourself," and "No greater love has a man than to lay down his life for his friends." This confirmed our ideas of unity and community, but we were not able to do it! The sacrifice required was too great for either of us to give up temporal pleasure now for the promise of some intangible happiness in the future.

On January 22, 1973, the U.S. Supreme Court declared that the "right" to murder unborn babies by abortion was guaranteed by the Constitution. Our motto, "Everything is for the children," required us to be pro-life—to respect, honor, and defend all human life. The first real glimmer of light entered our dull minds when we noticed that the Roman Catholic Church was the only organization on the planet that had been consistently against abortion, without compromise, for two thousand years! It was the most painful thing to realize because, more than anything else, we were decidedly anti-Catholic. "The Catholic Church can't be all bad," we had to admit, "because they are the only ones who will defend the innocent babies and call abortion murder." That was when we began to seriously consider the Catholic Church for the first time.

As soon as we began to question our anti-Catholic convictions, the movie *A Man for All Seasons*, about St. Thomas More and Henry VIII, was shown on television. After we watched the movie, someone said, "Let's take another look at that King James Bible." We had always used King James because it claimed to be the "Authorized Version"; we never touched the Catholic bibles because we had been told they were "censored." We read some history of sixteenth century England, and in a few weeks the Catholic Church began to shine—and suddenly the whole world turned upside down. There really *was* One Church founded by Jesus Christ, and it was not the church founded by Henry VIII which had published the "Authorized Bible." It was in fact, we began to realize, the same Church that Christ had promised to guide with "Another Comforter," the one built on Peter.

Two selfish Jews—stubborn, mean, proud, and ungrateful—being dragged, body and soul, by the Holy Spirit into the Light. It was a terrible battle, a battle with the Prince of Darkness himself, and it lasted three painful years even after we accepted Jesus as the Messiah. It was hell, but in the end it was friendship that claimed the victory.

It was the friendship of Jesus who freely gave his life for us and taught us by his example the way to love. It was the love of God reaching out to us through our mortal friends that finally moved my wife and me to embrace Jesus the Messiah wholeheartedly and be baptized in the Catholic Faith. God used the same friends we had met in 1968 to reveal his love and truth to us, and finally, the Holy Spirit opened our eyes—we saw others who sincerely loved the truth and were willing to give their lives for it. At last we knew that Jesus was our best friend. It was a shaky beginning, full of fear and sustained, it seemed, only by the sincere love of our friends, but we entered into the sacramental life of the Church, and God rewarded our timid commitment with Faith that grew stronger every day. After several years in the Church, we began to see clearly the realization of all our hopes and more—we had come home to where we all belonged.

The Catholic Church is universal: it has something for everyone, touching each of us in a very intimate way. We were impressed with the unbroken continuity between Judaism and Christianity; the Catholic Church *is* the Jewish Church. After studying Hebrew traditions from before Christ, we realized that, by following the Catholic teachings on sexuality and family life, we were living what Orthodox Judaism proscribed. The commandment to be fruitful and multiply had been followed long before Christianity, virginity was honored and respected, marriage was holy, and sex outside of marriage was a grave sin. The Judeo-Christian ethic always held the family as the basic unit of society, protected in every way by the religious customs, and "Honor your father and mother" was engraved in stone long before Christ.

Christ's instructions to feed the poor and care for the sick and homeless, etc., took on a new significance when we learned that he was following the ancient Hebrew traditions. We saw that Karl Marx, that false prophet whom we had revered, had taken all of his humanitarian programs from Jesus Christ himself, who was only articulating what God the Father had always instructed the Jews to do.

In the nineteenth century, the Catholic Church proclaimed the principles we should follow in organizing the production of material goods in order to insure the dignity and rights of individuals and families and still allow free initiative. These principles, set down by Pope Leo XIII in *Rerum Novarum*, were exactly the same principles my father fought for as a union leader when I was a child. It was a great joy to discover that it had all come from Christian social teaching (based on the Sermon on the Mount, on the whole Gospel) and not from Karl Marx as my father always taught me. Naturally I was disappointed when I tried to tell my parents about the source of all their humanitarian ideals, and they did not seem interested.

The common reaction of our fellow Jews towards those who become Christians is that only weak, stupid people would fall for such archaic and superstitious fantasy. This attitude accentuated our doubt and hesitation when we first entered the Church, so it was very consoling for us and a source of great strength to read about other twentieth century Jews who became Catholics—philosophers, scientists, doctors, rabbis, etc.—people who argued about the nature of God and could articulate their faith. We learned that the Catholic Faith is the most reasonable thing there is to believe; this is the greatest consolation of all—that our Faith is reasonable. (That is why we are now Dominicans, because Dominicans love reason.) We can explain our philosophy, our belief in the goodness of human life. We found the object of our search, we discovered the True Natural Law. As St. Peter says, "We must always be ready with a reason for the hope we have."

Looking back, Elasah and I are most grateful to God for his grace in our lives. We have now been happily married for sixteen years; we have eight wonderful children; our faith is alive, and is shared completely with our family; our lives have a structure and purpose that gives meaning and hope to all that we do. Grace works in many different ways, and we have seen grace change our lives in every aspect imaginable, but years ago we were not aware of God's intimate involvement in our affairs. Before we became Catholics we realized how crippled we were by sin, we wanted help, we desperately needed something. When we entered the Church we immediately began to get better: we saw grace coming from the Church through the sacraments and through the traditions of the Church, through the saints, through the Rosary; and we saw very clearly how grace came through other people, through our friends and through the many Catholics we met who helped us.

We wanted as much grace as we could get—who doesn't want as much of something for nothing as you can get? We read about the Third Order of St. Dominic and saw the tremendous grace it offered to lay people, so we became Third Order Dominicans and did in fact receive much grace thereby.

We found that it was not only possible for families to live in community but that the Church encouraged it. We received much grace from the traditions of the Church—going back to the Book of Acts and to the Hebrew traditions before Christ—in support of our effort to live in a lay community, and in fact we learned from Church history most of what we needed to make our community work.

The community we now live in, known as the St. Martin de Porres

Dominican Community, has sixty members and we are officially approved by the Dominican Order to live the common life. Our apostolic work of promoting Catholic family life and fighting against abortion has grown into one of the largest national pro-life organizations, and we now have our own complete print shop where we write, print, and distribute millions of pieces of literature yearly.

None of the members of the Community receives any salary for our apostolic work or works outside the Community. We are able to support ourselves entirely by printing and mailing literature for other Catholic pro-family organizations and by donations. We are very grateful to be able to do this because it gives us much time for our families and for each other and allows us to have a completely Catholic environment in which to raise our children. We have our own school here in the Community, and members of the Community do all the teaching.

We are very proud of our children, all of whom are happy, active, and hard working. They have formed their own apostolate, the Catholics United for Life Youth Crusaders, which teaches the value of purity and promotes the Confraternity of Angelic Warfare. They are invaluable teachers in our Sidewalk Counseling program and untiring workers in our pregnancy and counseling centers.

We are gratified to see our older community children now getting married and raising their own families with us, thus renewing the hope which our Community was originally founded upon. The founder of our Community has always said "Hope is worth about a billion dollars an ounce." We are indeed among the richest people to have ever walked the earth.

(Mark and Elasah welcome correspondence and are happy to answer questions about their conversion, their pro-life work, their life in a Catholic lay community, or whatever. Readers are invited to write them at Star Route Box 42, New Hope, Kentucky 40052.)

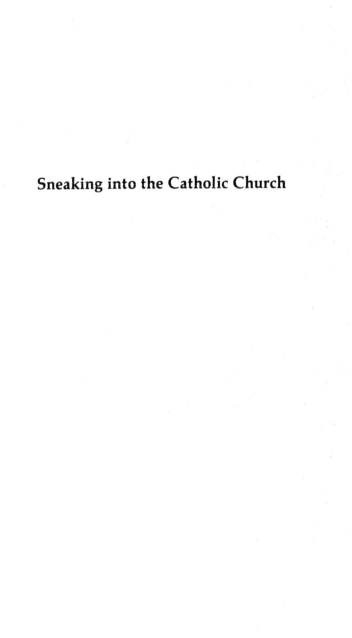

Sneaking into the Catholic Church

Gayle-Lynne Gordon

Sneaking into the Catholic Church

Gayle-Lynne Gordon

(Gayle-Lynne Gordon is a catechist and Secular Franciscan living and working in Los Angeles. She lives at home with her parents as a Catholic in a Jewish household. She is a registered nurse and also has a B.A. in history.)

*   *   *

Born in Chicago in 1950, but a Californian since 1959 when my father packed all of us, including the dog, into a station wagon, I come from a Reformed Jewish family. We are of Ashkenazi descent, which means we are Jews of Northern and Eastern European countries, as opposed to Sephardim of Mediterranian or Hispanic descent. I am a second generation American, with most of the family coming from Russia, Great Britain, France, and South Africa.

As Reformed Jews, our branch of Judaism is less concerned with rabbinical legalisms (such as keeping things kosher, etc.) and less rigid in religious observances and the use of Hebrew in the Temple service. How much is observed of rabbinic law can vary with the individual congregation.

Childhood

Growing up, my views about God changed considerably, which is a normal course of development. As a child, I saw God as a distant, stern, father-type, who was quick to anger and punishment. He chose my People to be His, whether or not they or I liked it. I was told that he was invisible, but, like any kid, I pictured him as an old man sitting on a throne in heaven.

Over the course of the years, God became closer and more real, and I came to realize that he was my friend, brother, teacher, guide, confidant. I began to consider my spiritual life as a journey or a walk with

God. I pictured him holding my hand on this walk, even during dark times.

Despite my strong sense of the spiritual life and my need for God, there was always a void in my life. As a Jew, I felt something was missing or unfulfilled. Even the Temple life and worship did not do much for me. There was a sense of boredom. Mind you, even with this feeling of unfulfillment, I at one time was to consider the possibility of training for the Rabbinate!

Perhaps I can explain the void, as I experienced it in youth, by explaining more about my own family's religious life. While they are Reform, they teeter on the edge of being Secular Jews. But they—and I—do have an identity as Jews. We share a deep pride in our history and our culture. We admire our people's tenacity in the face of severe adversity. We are well acquainted with the dreadful shame that comes from experiencing anti-Semitism. We love the State of Israel, and we support many charities.

But Judaism has many definitions, as can be seen from the still-raging debates about what the essence of being Jewish is. My family was not and is not actively religious. There is some distortion of authentic Jewish ethics, and God does not share a real place in our home.

My mother feels that one does not need to be religious, or know or love God, to be a good person. My mother *is* a good person, but she is not even certain of God's existence, and does not seem to care.

Like my mother, my father has a strong Jewish identity but has never really made his position concerning God known. He has a different idea about what Judaism teaches from the established ethics and doctrine. For example, he thinks that a Jew does not have to go out of his way to love his neighbor or to forgive him. He thinks that forgiveness is a limited thing. In fact, in his eyes, my attempts at peacemaking are a Christian thing only.

We have had limited religious observances within the home. My folks sent me and my brothers to religious school; both my brothers went to Hebrew school and were "Bar Mitzvahed." Although I did not study any Hebrew, I went through many years of religious education. Sometimes it was a real bore for me, and I would fight my parents tooth and nail about going. Despite my reluctance, though, I did enjoy many of my classes and was a good student.

I went through Judaic studies until two years past my Confirmation. Confirmation is primarily a Reform innovation which occurs around the age of sixteen. By it, one says "yes" to Judaism and is blessed by God, the Rabbi, and the local congregation.

In the story of my gradual coming toward Christ in the days of my youth, I feel a lot had to do with my living in a "mixed" neighborhood in Chicago, where I grew up before the move to California. "Mixed" meant for me living in an area which was both Gentile and Jewish.

In my apartment building, the vast majority of the Gentile kids were Catholics, and many of these were my playmates. One of our play activities was having make-believe weddings. As I remember it, each of us children had a part to play: the bride, the groom, the priest, family, and friends. I recall that the bride and groom exchanged their vows in a celebration of the "sacrament" of matrimony, witnessed by their priest, family, and friends. It was a double ring ceremony, and we even went so far as to have a reception afterwards, with cake and the usual refreshments. After that, the "happy couple" left on their honeymoon!

This pretend wedding was held annually on a warm summer day at my apartment complex, and was fully participated in, not only by our neighborhood kids, but by our parents as well. The event was planned and staged in a very theatrical way. I usually played the groom (ah. . . never the bride!), but sometimes, if I was lucky, I got to play the priest, wearing very makeshift vestments, but never consecrating a host. That was the role to be envied!

I think that when some of your play activity involves the Church, though in a seemingly unimportant way, you can't help but be curious about it. And I was curious in a big way! I recall asking my friends questions such as why they ate fish on Friday.

Besides having intellectual discussions—as intellectual as one can get at a young age—I did something else. Just for the fun of it, I used to sneak into the local Catholic church. I do not recall exactly how this game started, but I am sure that my friends were a great influence—

perhaps they dared me, but I don't remember. Nevertheless, I did go into the church, and I thought it was a great game!

There were not any guard towers or anything to sneak past (sorry about that, but I did have quite an imagination), but the excitement was in being in the church without my parents' knowledge or approval, and most of all, in not letting the Catholics know. After all, I thought to myself, who knows what they might say or do if they found out a non-Catholic was in their midst! Also, it would have spoiled my fun if I did not feel I was sneaking in.

Not only was it thrilling to sneak in, undiscovered, but I very much enjoyed the liturgy. It was as good as seeing a movie to me. Because it was so different from what I was used to, I found it entertaining. I also enjoyed my own participation—I found I could kneel with the best of those Catholics; I was becoming a master of imitation.

If you thought I was good at pretending to be a Catholic at Masses, you should have seen me at Communion. My first Communion was obtained in perhaps an illicit manner. As a child, I underwent a series of eye muscle surgeries. On one of my trips to the hospital, I had a Catholic roommate. She was being prepared by a priest for her First Holy Communion. During our hospitalization, I would read her Missal; in fact, I even fell asleep with it, and while I slept, I was blessed by the good Father. The next day, when he came to give her the Eucharist, I remember kneeling in my bed too. For some reason unclear to me, except to say that my ability to imitate was at the highest level, the priest gave me Holy Communion. My roommate did not spoil the fun by giving me away.

For years I would sneak Communion, and, even though she was not a Catholic, my good friend Marjorie would have fits when I did it. After all, I did not believe in the reality of the Eucharist. I did not even believe in Christ. For a long time, I was actually dismayed by the apparent cannibalism of my Catholic friends—they were saying that this was the *Body* of Christ. How could that be done, without offending my sensibilities? But you would be absolutely incorrect if you assumed that this would deter me from my game. Perhaps it was one of the many ways in which the Holy Spirit was reaching me.

In my childhood, I had also fallen in love with Christmas. It was (and is) my favorite holiday, followed by Halloween. I loved these more than any Jewish holidays, and since many Jewish children feel the same way, I will try to help you understand.

My strongest memory of Passover, which I still celebrate with my family today, was of sitting and starving through three-hour-long Seders at my grandparents' house. We were celebrating the Hebrews' escape to freedom from their Egyptian oppressors—and I sure hoped that they didn't starve the way I had to.

By contrast, Christmas held a lot of wonder, and this Jewish child wanted Christmas very badly. I felt I was the only one who was so deprived, not because I was interested in the Christ Child, but because I wanted the trappings.

I wanted Christmas, and I was going to have it. I remember arguing and begging my parents for it, but naturally they said "No!" and occasionally they explained why not. But that didn't hold water for me, and I felt that their arguments were not logical—after all, as a young child I had been taken to see Santa Claus!

So, I figured that my folks could not say no if I already had the stuff; once again I had to take on a life of crime. I was not going to be deprived of what my friends had, so I actually stole some branches from a neighbor's tree. I placed the branches in a glass milk bottle and decorated them with makeshift ornaments made from construction paper. Then I put my presents under the "tree"; it was a bit sparse, but was truly effective. And what could my parents say?

As a Beverly Hills resident, I was not so Catholic-oriented. There were no "bad influences" (friends), nor were there Roman Catholic churches I could easily get to. And at this time, I was going through a "Jewish and darn stubborn about it" period, so I was not going about in the middle of the night to steal trees.

Once we moved to the San Fernando Valley, however, I made some good Christian friends, and so my hankering for Christmas redeveloped. To solve that problem, I began to go over to friends' homes for the holidays. And once my Dad even allowed a real Christmas tree—whoops, I mean Chanukah Bush—into the house, and we had lights outside. What a glorious year! (To this day, my brothers, who are not Christian, have Christmas decorations in their homes every year.

Maybe they had better be careful—who knows what that could lead to!)

In my own case, I can see now that I was being gently led, although I did not always know it or want it. I suppose the desire for the Christmas holiday atmosphere could be called symptomatic of my Christian leanings.

During my "Jewish and proud of it" period, I still did not go frequently to religious services, but I did go to some of the High Holy Day services, as well as those required by the Heder (religious school) curriculum. In addition, I was head over heels in love with our Rabbi. I had an affection for him beyond the strictly religious sense. When I took his classes, I surely paid careful attention to him, but it wasn't just for his rabbinical wisdom—he was handsome.

It was to this Rabbi that I confided my own desire to become a rabbi. He gave me good support and also understood my search for answers to questions about my faith. I have to admit, however, that the Roman Catholic sympathies were probably still there: when the good Rabbi one day made a Catholic joke in class (in good taste), he jokingly asked that all the Catholics leave before he told it—and I stood up to leave. Everyone thought it was terribly witty of me.

With all my Christian leanings, why did I not make the switch until much later? For several reasons: I was still underage, I was very stubborn, and I did not at this time really have a true sense of who Christ was. And there was another problem, caused by something ugly which I had both studied and experienced: anti-Semitism, with it's extreme inhumanity as evidenced in the Holocaust.

Anti-Semitism has occurred for centuries, and it is very real. I experienced it as a child. I remember being called a "Christ Killer," and one day being cornered into a brick cul-de-sac of our building in Chicago and being struck by boys twice my age and height—they called me some filthy things. These incidents, as well as a strong acquaintance with the history of anti-Semitism, were enough for me to harbor some ill feelings. How could one want to convert to Christ when some Christian groups mistreated others? I thought Christians were told to "love your neighbor," not hate them, and I felt I was certainly a neighbor.

Last year, I appeared on *Heart of the Nation,* a Catholic television show, and I was asked why there aren't more conversions from Judaism to the Church. I bluntly said that one reason was the trauma of anti-Semitism. The priest on the show thought that was of such importance, that he discussed it more in his homily. I am sure that the show shook up a few Catholics and non-Catholics alike who might harbor such bigotry.

Thank God for Vatican II and Pope John XXIII for not only renewing the Church, but for also beginning to address the issue of religious prejudice more strongly in order to correct the great wrong which the Church admits she had a part in. I really think that if Vatican II had not taken place and the Church had not begun moving into still greater articulation of the need for love for Jews and others, I probably would never have converted, despite my leanings toward Christianity.

Coming Closer

The greatest influence in my life toward Christianity during my young adulthood was my Protestant friend, Marjorie. How she nagged the Lord about me! She was always having religious discussions with me and would quote Scripture to me, especially Psalm 22 with its Christological content. Even when I fought her tooth and nail, she would persist in prayer and discussion.

I had another Protestant friend whom God sent to me. Out of friendship and love, Doug would nag me about Christianity. He was concerned that, come Judgment Day, I would be cast into the Pit if I had not brought Christ into my life as Savior. But my attitude to him was "I don't bother you—don't bother me!" I felt that people were entitled to follow their respective faiths without being coerced by others. Doug came from a Protestant tradition, and I was becoming decidedly Judeo-Catholic. So, despite any readiness I might have had, comments like Doug's would cause me, in my stubbornness, to stop dead in my tracks.

What Doug and Marge did not know at the time was that, on my own, I had begun to sneak back into church, and I was actually reading up on what they were both preaching to me about. I was finally accepting the fact that Jesus was a historical person. I had come to believe that he was a great Rabbi and perhaps a prophet. I was beginning to accept his teachings slowly. Acceptance of him as God, Savior, however, took a while longer.

Enter Richard Burton, an actor I enjoyed very much. In the 1960s Burton made a wonderful movie based on a play about the medieval English Chancellor, Archbishop, and Martyr Saint, Thomas à Becket. After seeing this film on television and, having an inquisitive mind and a love for history, I began to read all I could get my hands on about the real saint.

My interest in Becket inspired me to make several pilgrimages to Canterbury. There I discovered that, if you are not a member of the Church, or if you have fallen away, if you pray to St. Thomas, he will bring you to the Church. In my case, I am sure he had a hand in my eventual conversion. In fact, a woman whom I met through my interest in St. Thomas later became my confirmation sponsor.

Slowly, with the help of St. Thomas, I was learning to overcome doubts and hurts. During this period, I recall needing spiritual comfort after one of the Kennedy brothers was shot. I was very upset and needed someplace to go; as I did not live close to the Temple, I went over to the local parish church. While sitting before the Tabernacle, I felt a great sense of Presence—a Presence that was very real to me. From then on, I got into the habit of making frequent visits there, and, after a while, became known by the pastor as his "Jewish parishioner."

Baptism

Still, it took more time for the Spirit to change me. My friend Marge goaded me on. Confused by my "dabbling" in Catholicism, she urged me to make up my mind and stop sneaking around. It was not until 1973, however, that I finally decided to declare myself a Christian. Marge was overjoyed.

Now I needed to get baptized. I met with the new associate of the parish and we discussed my feelings and knowledge of the Faith at length. I still remember his asking me if I knew what I was letting myself in for—I did!

I wanted to be baptized on Trinity Sunday, but instead was baptized along with some other adults and an infant during the Mass on

Pentecost Sunday, June 2, 1974, at St. Francis de Sales Church in Sherman Oaks. I reverently received the Eucharistic Lord for the first time (legally). My mother came to the baptism late and in tears. My father did not come at all.

One night, three weeks before my baptism, as we were walking our dogs, I had told my father about my intent. He seemed very understanding and said he could always see it coming and that he had felt it was only a matter of time. But after my baptism, the understanding of my parents disappeared. My mother even now begs me to give up the Church. She feels ashamed and worries about our relatives and friends finding out.

Despite the ill feeling I experienced from my family, I still made it to Confirmation. Gayle being Gayle, I did raise a few eyebrows. You see, I was determined to take the name of my patron, Thomas à Becket. That caused quite a stir. I had to get special permission from the Chancery in order to take a male saint's name as part of my own. But the Cardinal never batted an eye when he confirmed me Thomas on November 4, 1974, at Good Shepherd Church in Beverly Hills.

I have been in the Church thirteen years now, and in that time I have become more and more grateful to my Messiah for my conversion. But conversion does not stop with baptism—it is a lifelong process of turning toward God. It is a daily falling and rising with Christ.

In the years since my baptism, I have matured more in my faith and have seen many changes. I am far from being the perfect Christian, but the Lord has helped me all along the way, teaching me many important lessons.

I have come to realize that I did not leave Judaism but have completed it and, in the last few years, I have reached out to other Hebrew-Catholics, sharing my faith in Christ as well as our common heritage.

The Lord can take negative situations and make them positive: because of the prejudices of others, I have studied more about my faith and have since become a catechist and can preach the Good News to others. The ministry renews me and gives me much happiness, and I share the Jewish roots common to all of us with those I teach.

So, despite the bad times, I thank God for the good times and have never regretted my conversion. It took years to conclude that the void I felt was the lack of a Messiah. The Church has brought me full circle to realize my Jewishness as well as my Christianity.

By the way, my friend Marjorie has since become a Catholic and is my god-child!

I will leave you all with a short prayer and blessing:

May the Lord help us to understand one another,
And guide us all, each on his or her personal journey.
And,
May the Lord bless you and keep you.
May He shine His face upon you,
And give you all Peace.

Pax et Bonum.

A Chasid in the Heart of the Church

Charles Rich with Ronda Chervin

A Chasid in the Heart of the Church

Charles Rich

(Charles Rich is a lay contemplative living in a Jesuit House. He is the author of Reflections *(St. Bede's, 1986), made up of articles originally published in* Our Sunday Visitor, *and of* The Embrace of the Soul: Meditations on the Song of Songs *(St. Bede's, 1984). This short account of his conversion is taken from the Introduction to* Reflections. *It is in the form of a letter to his spiritual director. It should be added that Charles Rich was brought up in a small village in Hungary within a Chasidic community. Much given to contemplation, he would spend hours in the forests, even as a small boy, communing with God. As a youth, the family moved to New York City where he lost his faith in Judaism.)*

*   *   *

Dear Father,

I am very much afraid that what you ask of me is impossible. How can I tell you what made me become a Catholic; how can I ever hope to put down on paper all that went on in my mind and heart up to the time of my conversion? What I can do is to repeat again some of the things about myself with which you are already familiar. You know, for instance, that I was raised in a strictly orthodox Jewish environment, that I had been deeply instructed in the faith of my people, and that all this training had been completely worn away by the time I had reached the age of fourteen. From then on I looked elsewhere for spiritual nutriment, in the field of culture and education.

The more culture and education I acquired, however, the more conscious I became that these would never fill the gap which the loss of my religious faith had left. It was this realization which was responsible for my preoccupation during the course of many years with the faiths and beliefs of other people, preoccupations which ultimately led me into the writings of Catholicism.

Here in Catholicism I discovered a world molded along lines which were closest to the desires of my heart; here I found a view of life which satisfied the many sides of my nature. I began to read all the great writers I could find on Catholicism, from St. Augustine's "City of God" to Karl Adam's "Spirit of Catholicism." In these books I found living waters at which I quenched my thirst for the supernatural and the Divine, a thirst which was implanted in me ever since I can remember.

Influenced as I became by the spirit of these writings, I still felt very far from the kind of Catholicism which I now know since my conversion. There were far too many qualifications to be made, too many difficulties to be overcome for me to have felt entirely at home in it. It was one thing to see the land of peace from the mountain's shaggy top and to find a way thither, and another to essay through ways unassailable and to keep on the way that leads thither.

In the meantime, my spiritual and intellectual life became anarchic and chaotic; I did not know where I was, what I believed or where I stood on any matter. I felt that something desperate had to be done if I would avert spiritual suicide. I read the New Testament and tried to fathom the full meaning of Our Lord's sayings. I felt that there was something about these utterances with which I was deeply in sympathy and which was different from anything ever spoken by a human being, different in tone from the utterances of the great poets I admired so much. There was a note of hope in them, of confidence and trust which became medicinal to a mind tormented and distracted by anxiety and doubt. But in spite of the healing influence which the reading of the Gospel writings had upon me, there was yet, I felt, something vitally lacking. I was still searching. Christ had not yet become God to me. I regarded Him as but a man, a supereminently perfect and august man, this and no more. I was still under the influence of the view which Renan and the rationalist school represented. I sought elsewhere for God.

I went to Spinoza. For two years, I was under the complete sway and influence of this man's mind. His Ethics had become a Bible to me. I began to worship him as a saint. The mere sound of his name would thrill me with joy. He became to me the divine, the blessed, the truly "God-intoxicated" Spinoza. And all this while I did not realize that I was worshipping a weak human being, as feeble and helpless as myself.

This drunken fury with the doctrines of pantheism lasted, as I have mentioned, for over two years. The whole universe became Spinozistic. God became everything and nothing. He was everywhere and nowhere, and I awoke from this hallucination to find myself more miserable than ever. Spinozism had failed to remove the doubt, the torment, and the anxiety that oppressed my mind; its charm faded completely, its doctrines became cold and lifeless.

What was I to do now? Where was I to turn with any hope? I lost faith in all philosophy. I turned in my desperation to the writings of the mystics, to Eckhart, to Bohme, to Plotinus, and Emerson, but here I met with even greater disappointment. Under the maze of confused words which concealed their doctrines, lay nothing but obscurity and darkness. The further I waded into them, the more hopelessly entangled everything became; they only led me deeper into the darkness from which I sought to emerge.

I withdrew from my acquaintances also. They were themselves too miserable to be able to afford comfort to others. And to look to them for guidance or help would be like asking the blind to lead the blind.

One day while I was passing a church, the thought occurred to me to go in and rest a while; perhaps this would bring some relief to my mind. It was not my first visit to a Catholic church; I had often been in one before, but it was the first time that I went into one with the hope of finding in there something which I could find nowhere else. And as I sat in the peace and quiet of that atmosphere, these thoughts kept running through my mind:

If only I could believe with the same assurance as those who come to worship here believe! If I could only believe that the words in the Gospels are really true, that Christ really existed, and that these words are exactly those that came from His own mouth, were uttered from His own human lips, and that they are literally true. Oh, if this were only a fact, if I could only believe that this were a fact, how glorious and wonderful that would be, how consoled, happy, and comforted I would be, to know and to believe that Christ was really Divine, that He was God's own Son come down from another world to this earth to save us all! Could it be possible, I felt, that that which seemed too wonderful to be true actually was true, that it was no deception, no fraud, no lie? All of a sudden something flashed through my mind and I heard these words spoken in it. "Of course it is true, Christ is God, is God come down to make Himself visible in the flesh. The words in the Gospels are true, literally true."

The next thing I remember was that I found myself on my knees in fervent prayer and thanksgiving. I felt a deep gratitude in my heart for something which made me feel very happy, but what it was I could not say. All that I know is that, from that day on, the name of Our Lord Jesus Christ took on a significance which it never before had. There was an ineffable fragrance about the words *Jesus Christ*, a sweetness with which nothing can be compared. The sound of these words to this day fills me with a strange inexpressible joy, a joy which I feel does not come from this world.

It was not long after this that I saw an announcement of a series of conferences to be given by you at the Fordham University Chapel. The title, "The Mystical Christ and the Modern World," immediately captured my imagination, and I resolved to hear you the following Sunday. It was soon after this that the thought of entering the Church seriously entered my mind. I was spiritually homeless, and what better thing could I do than to ally myself with a people with a whole viewpoint with which I already had so much in common? I could accept Christ, then why not Catholicism also? After hearing you say that the Catholic Church was "Jesus Christ diffused and communicated," I was convinced that the next logical step was to embrace Catholicism.

But no sooner had I arrived at this decision than thousands of difficulties began to present themselves. It would take too long now to enter into the nature of these. Thanks to God's grace, they were all successfully met.

When some of my friends learned of this intention of mine to enter the Catholic Faith, they assumed a very abusive and hostile attitude toward me. Some even went so far as to warn me of serious mental disturbances unless I immediately desisted from preoccupying myself with Catholic writings. I was forfeiting, they warned me, all sound reason and I had better wake up. This made me very sad, for I knew from what ignorance and blindness they spoke. Most of them never read a good Catholic book in their lives; their knowledge of Catholicism rested on the flimsiest sort of material gathered from wild hearsay and rumor, and the truth of the following words came forcibly home to me: "Religion has nothing more to fear than not being properly understood." It was their essential ignorance of the profound Catholic teachings that made them hate me for my willingness to embrace these teachings. It was ignorance and ignorance alone that spoke in them.

One evening while riding home on the subway, perplexed by doubt, just after having had a bitter dispute with one of my friends, the consequences of which filled me with an unbearable grief, suddenly in the midst of all this despair and darkness I felt an unaccountable feeling of happiness come over me and flood my whole inner being with joy almost heavenly. Grief instantly left me, and my anxieties and doubts vanished as if by a miracle. I knew and felt from that minute that I would be able to overcome all the obstacles in the way of my accepting Catholicism. And I did overcome them. By the aid of His Light which came to me, the road became easier and easier, and on the feast of St. Cyril of Jerusalem, March 18, 1933, I was formally received into the Church.

From then on there is little to be said. I have, since my Baptism and First Communion, acquired a happiness which I would not exchange for anything in all the world. It has given to me a peace of mind and a serenity of outlook which I did not think was possible on this earth. All my anxieties, doubts, and mental torments have completely left me, and I am for the first time in many years at peace with myself and with the world. I suppose the Buddhist would characterize this sort of peace by the word *Nirvana*, but I would much prefer to call it by the familiar language of Paul: "The peace of God that surpasses all understanding."

Discovering the Father

Raphael Simon, OCSO

Discovering the Father

Raphael Simon, O.C.S.O.

(Raphael Simon is a medical doctor and psychiatrist who entered the Catholic Church more than fifty years ago at the age of twenty-seven. He became a Trappist four years later in 1940 and has belonged to his present community since then. He was ordained a priest in 1947. He has been a spiritual director, retreat master, and director of centering prayer workshops.

He is the author of The Glory of Thy People: A Conversion Story, *and* Hammer and Fire: Way to Contemplative Happiness, Fruitful Ministry, and Mental Health, *which explains the spiritual life and its mental health value. Both of these books have been published by St. Bede's Publications, Petersham, Massachusetts.)*

*　　　*　　　*

Born in 1909 in New York City of Reformed Jewish parents, I entered the University of Michigan at the age of sixteen. I had a desire to know the truth, and after two years of scattered courses, I sensed a lack of unity in what I was learning. In 1929 I went to the University of Berlin, Germany, hoping to find something that seemed to be lacking in my studies in the United States.

At Berlin, I found in philosophy the possibility of the unity of knowledge. I had a sense that in philosophy there could be found an inner kingdom of truth and justice which corresponded to what I was seeking. I also developed an interest in psychiatry as a vocation which I thought might offer me the opportunity to pursue philosophic study.

Since high school days, I had lost my perception of God and had drifted into agnosticism. Nevertheless, God gave me the desire to find the truth and Him who is the Truth, and led me to philosophy as an avenue for doing so, and to a vocation as a psychiatrist.

If I wished to be a psychiatrist, I had to enter medical school and also complete premedical science courses. One of the doctors who was interviewing applicants for the University of Michigan Medical School asked me what courses I had taken, and I explained apologetically that I had had a lot of liberal arts courses, including philosophy. I thought this would be considered a liability in a medical school candidate by this down-to-earth surgeon. But his response was that a broader educational background was of value to a doctor. I was accepted.

It was during my fourth undergraduate year at Michigan that I met two other students who likewise lived in New York City. In fact, the three of us lived within ten or fifteen blocks of each other in Manhattan. We might not have met at all but for the fact that we were all on the same bus going to New York for Christmas. These students were Herbert Ratner and Herbert Schwartz, who were to play an important part in my life.

Herbert Schwartz and I entered medical school together. Herbert Ratner, then in the Bacteriology Department, entered the next year. After my sophomore year, I spent a year doing research in the Department of Materia Medica (Pharmacology), and so it was that Herbert Ratner and I graduated in the same class in 1934. Herbert Schwartz dropped out of medical school the first year and instead went to Columbia University, where he obtained a Ph.D. in philosophy under Professor Richard McKeon, with whom I was to study.

I had hoped that psychiatric practice, which would give me the opportunity to help people, would also provide me with the income and time to pursue philosophic study—in search of this inner kingdom of justice and truth. During the summer between my junior and senior years of medical school, I had an externship in psychiatry at the Pontiac State Hospital. There I wrestled with the call to an active vocation of helping people through psychiatric practice and a contemplative vocation of searching for the truth through philosophy. I felt that a combination of these, such as I was planning, would best meet these desires.

In my final year of medical school, I was introduced to the philosophy of Aristotle and Thomas Aquinas by Herbert Schwartz who conducted a class for me and two others. He had come to Aristotle and

Thomas while pursuing his doctoral studies in philosophy—studies inclusive of the modern philosophers.

As this last year in medical school progressed, I had an opportunity to enter more quickly and intensely into the study of philosophy. Robert Maynard Hutchins, the President of the University of Chicago, had called Mortimer Adler to that University. Then he enlisted Richard McKeon and Herbert Schwartz, McKeon's brilliant student. William Gorman, another friend of mine, also obtained a post there. I obtained a grant to work with Professor McKeon on research in the philosophy of medicine. So in the Fall of 1934, we three friends— Schwartz, Gorman, and myself—were together at the University of Chicago.

President Hutchins was a remarkable person. At the age of twenty-eight he was a successful Dean of the Yale Law School. As President of the University of Chicago, he spoke and wrote about "the intellectual love of God." He believed that theology should be the center of a great university, and philosophy should be the medium of communication. One same philosophy would provide for a common understanding and rational center of unity, something I had found so missing in my first two years at college and in the contemporary world, where pluralism makes mutual understanding and deeper communication so difficult. In this atmosphere all the modern disciplines could be more fruitfully cultivated, with interdisciplinary relatedness, enhancing each other and overcoming the alienating effects of specialization, without losing its benefits. This presupposed that there was one true philosophy, demonstrable as such, and that it could be widely accepted. Here was a plan for that unity of knowledge in education which I had been seeking.

The philosophy which Hutchins held to be the true one was the philosophy of Aristotle. It had been recognized as such by Thomas Aquinas, who further developed it along the lines of its own inner logic. That is why Adler, McKeon, Schwartz, Gorman, myself, and a number of others, who were Aristotelians, and each a specialist in a modern discipline, were gathered here together at the University of Chicago.

I was accorded the rank of a research assistant in the History

Department, and then in my second year in Chicago, research associate with rank of instructor in the Medical School.

A number of students, mostly those from the Honors Course taught by Hutchins and Adler, and some of the Aristotelians, used to gather almost nightly at Herbert Schwartz's for conversation about philosophy.

This was a very beautiful time in my life, calm and peaceful. In it I experienced a rich intellectual and moral development. Herbert, Bill Gorman, and I were constantly together, and, besides the group of perhaps twenty persons who met at Herbert's evenings, there was an outer circle of young single and married people with whom we had a less close, but also meaningful association.

Most of us were Jews or Protestants. Our conversation in the smaller and larger circles was philosophic, not religious or theological, and I am not aware of any religious practice on the part of those with whom we associated. Nevertheless, I am sure that these men and women were especially beloved by the Father, both those who eventually entered the Catholic Church, and those who did not do so. They were upright, sincere, moral people, interested in their studies and academic pursuits.

In *The Glory of Thy People*, in the scope of some 135 pages, I have sketched the development of insights drawn from the philosophy we studied and discussed. I have indicated there the moral and spiritual progress which prepared me for the signal grace of the faith which God gratuitously gave me; grace preparing for grace, all a free and loving gift of the Father, leading to an increasing freedom of heart and to a mind more conscious of the unity of all truth. I will not repeat that account.

But something of the nature of my search for truth, I will try to communicate. It was not a love of antiquity, a desire to return to the past or to reconstruct some former period. It was simply a search for truth.

I had discovered the great philosophic achievement of Aristotle, who had benefited from the work of Plato and Socrates. I found that Thomas Aquinas had further developed the work of Plato and Aristotle. This elaboration of philosophic truth was a peak which is certainly surpassable and open to further development, but which has not been equalled.

Aristotle was a great natural investigator, founder of the modern sciences (his work also made provision for the mathematical sciences), who had taught that human authority was the weakest of all props on which to base a conclusion. Thomas contented himself in his major philosophic works with writing commentaries on, explanations of, Aristotle's works. He called him "the philosopher." The key to the deep understanding of Aristotle in my teachers at Chicago was their knowledge of Thomas' exposition of Aristotle.

It was a very happy discovery which in my third year of undergraduate study at the age of eighteen led me to see in philosophy the hope of a unified understanding of truth, and, as a consequence, an interest in philosophy which brought me upon graduation from medical school to the enterprise I was now engaged in at Chicago. I was in the midst of a stimulating movement—it was a renaissance. There had been such a renaissance in England in the nineteenth century at Oxford University called the Oxford Movement, which had been broader, more long-lasting, and involved more people. And whereas theirs had been a renaissance of patristics and religion, ours was of philosophy.

While I had discovered that philosophy was a way to truth, and to the unity and consistency of truth, I was not unappreciative of science. What I found dissatisfying was not the scientific method or its fruits, but fragmented, dissociated knowledge, and the lack of a unifying or interrelating discipline. Modern philosophy had not supplied that lack: the philosohy of Whitehead, of the pragmatists, of the idealists, of Schopenhauer, and of Nietzsche. The modern philosophies were very much at variance with each other, and, I felt, at variance also with reality.

What Aristotle's philosophy, perfected by Thomas, offered was a philosophy based on common sense and empirically known reality. All knowledge, for them, starts with the senses. But it does not stop there. Truth depends on the truth of the premises and the correctness of reasoning from these premises. Reason, starting from what is observed and known through the senses, can draw conclusions which lead to insight into even non-material reality, such as God, the first cause of all material being.[1]

Not everything held by Aristotle is true. Nevertheless, he worked out basic philosophic truth which helps to solve modern philosophic dilemmas.[2] What helped me to appreciate Aristotle was that in thinking over the matters he was treating, I could come by myself to what I would later find him teaching. And my teachers, trained in the school of Aristotle and Thomas, were themselves powerful reasoners and thinkers. I had not met their equal elsewhere.

Modern thought is heavily weighted with the brilliant errors made by a succession of modern thinkers. These errors are invested in the negative precepts of modern science. Its positive precepts are entirely in accord with the philosophy of Aristotle and Thomas, and are even a worthwhile development, which accounts for the success of modern science. The task, I thought, was to combine and support modern disciplines with the perennial truths of philosophy. Philosophy provided a check for examining the unconscious philosophic assumptions of scientists, who stepped outside the field of their competence in making philosophic statements as if they were scientific truths.

Since my studies were thus a critique of modern thought in the light of perennial philosophy, the prejudices of my contemporaries showed more clearly, by contrast, Thomas' awareness and frank statement of his own presuppositions. I could no longer consider the religion which this great thinker explained and defended in his works to be something unworthy of a critical modern intelligence. I had no intention at the moment of examining Thomas' theology, but my prejudices against it were offset by my appreciation of his probity of mind.

At this juncture, I read the Gospel. This was a bold undertaking for a Jew. It was being discussed in the Honors Course as one of the Great Books to which contemporary civilization is heir. In reading it, a comment of President Hutchins proved meaningful. He said that if one wanted *to make sense* of the Bible, one should read it as if it were true. He did not say that it *was* true, but that reading if as if it were true would help to understand it. Perhaps this was in my mind when, in order to give the Gospel a fair reading, I bracketed for later reflection those elements in it which touched on my sensibilities and prejudices—

for example, the miracles. This permitted a more critical reading than if I had allowed my antagonistic emotions to interfere with an intelligent perusal of the text.

What I found was a narrative told unimpassionedly, a drama unfolding among characters whom I could identify with those in my current experience. Jesus, with his flaying, cutting rejoinders to his enemies, did not fit my ideal of the wise, balanced man who "followed in all things the golden mean." But much less could I identify with his enemies. As the story unfolded, I became aware of the beauty of the personality of Jesus and its power and authority. Where did such authority, such brilliance, come from? I could not attribute it to the editors of the Gospels or the milieu from which they came. I could not account for it as being purely human. I realized that in this drama, so true to life in a way that defied human artistry or ingenuity alone to explain, I was forced to take sides and not remain a mere spectator.

Under these circumstances, I read the Apostles' Creed to see what it was that the Catholic Church held. I could not find in it anything that my knowledge or reason could disprove.

The second time that I read the Gospel of St. John, and came to Easter Sunday when Christ entered through closed doors the upper room where His Jewish apostles were gathered, I realized that I believed. Jesus had come through the closed doors of my heart, doors which had been as securely closed to Him as are the doors of any materialistic scientist. He had given me the gift of Faith.

After this, I took a period of time each day to do spiritual reading and to pray. I read St. Augustine's commentary on the Gospel according to St. John, Msgr. Fulton Sheen's *The Mystical Body of Christ* (St. Paul's phrase for the Church), and, later, the Baltimore Catechism—this activity on my part was unknown to anyone.

It was as if the heavens had opened and light and joy streamed in, and it was only a few months later that I approached a priest, Father Gillis, C.S.P. in New York City, to ask for Baptism, just prior to my departure for Europe. He bade me to come back at the end of the summer, and when I did so, he referred me to the pastor of the parish in Chicago where I was returning in September, saying that I would need instructions to prepare for Baptism. So it was that I was instructed and baptized by Father Joseph Connerton in St. Thomas the Apostle Church—the parish church of the University of Chicago—on November 6, 1936. My experience, like that of many others from all types of backgrounds, was an experience of coming home—and of being at home. My entrance into the Catholic Church was a shock to my mother. She called me a traitor. At her request, eight months after my entrance into the Church, I returned to New York where she and my father lived. My poor dear mother, whose fault was that she loved her son too much, wrote that if I did so, she would make no effort to draw me out of the Church. In response to her wish, and after making a novena to the Holy Spirit for light at my director's advice, I did return to New York, obtaining a psychiatric internship at Bellevue, through the recommendation of the head of the Michael Reese Hospital's Psychiatric Department, Dr. Jascha Kasanin, a Jewish psychoanalyst with whom I had become friends after my conversion, and who was thrilled by the reasons I gave for it. Thus, during the next few years, I was able to spend every other weekend with my mother and father. To do this was one of the motives of my returning to New York, for I realized that since the age of sixteen I had been away from home, except for vacations, and I owed my mother and father this companionship.

My dad and I spent some delightful times together, driving around the perimeter of Manhattan, attending together the lectures of Father Walter Farrell, O.P., and so on.

During the next four years I held various positions, interning at the Oak Park Hospital, the Bellevue Psychiatric Hospital in New York City, and the Brooklyn State (psychiatric) Hospital. After this, I was psychiatrist at Lincoln Hall, Lincolndale in Westchester County, a modern rehabilitation institution for delinquent boys from New York City, run by the Christian Brothers. But in the midst of all of this, I found myself drawn to the religious life and the priesthood, and so I entered the Trappist Cisterican Order in Our Lady of the Valley monastery, Valley Falls, Rhode Island, on December 8, 1940. This monastery, after a disastrous fire in 1950, moved to Spencer, Massachusetts and adopted the name of St. Joseph's Abbey.

When my mother first came with my father to visit me at the

monastery, shortly after my entrance, she said, "Bud, your relatives think that you are in a mental hospital, and I would rather have them think that than that you are at a monastery, so I haven't told them!"

Shortly after this, her father, an orthodox Jew, died in San Diego, without ever having learned of my conversion. While she was in California, my father died of a heart attack.

Several years later, when I was in St. Joseph's Hospital in Providence, critically ill, she walked into the room, put her hands on her hips and, looking me in the face, said, "What do you mean dying before I do—haven't you caused me enough suffering already?!"

On one occasion, when I came out to the visiting parlor at the monastery to see my mother, she referred to the crucifix on the opposite wall and said, "I'm contemplating Jesus on the cross." On another occasion, referring to the picture of St. Therese on the frontispiece of her autobiography in the monastery Gift Shop, Mother said, "She's so beautiful, the Catholic religion must be true." And while waiting for me to come out for a visit, at this same Gift Shop, she told a lady who wanted a priest to bless a religious article she had just bought, "Wait for my son, he'll bless it!"

Despite all this, we rarely spoke about religion. However, on one visit, while I was driving Mother around the neighborhood, she said, "Bud, I can't understand how Catholics worship three Gods." I explained that we worship one God, the same God as the Jews worship, who made the Jews His chosen people, but that Jesus, God's Son, revealed that there were three Persons in the one God: Himself, the Image of the Father, and the Holy Spirit, the Love that proceeds from them, who is Himself a Person.

On another visit, a black seminarian from Boston was telling me, in her presence, how confused and upset he was by racial prejudice in the seminary. I told him that I had met racial prejudice too. Although I believed myself a Jew, more completely a Jew because I had accepted the Jewish Messiah whom other Jews awaited, when I prayed, I was only conscious of Christ whom I loved, and didn't know then whether I was black or white, Gentile or Jew—nothing mattered except Christ. After all, what color is the soul? As I explained this, I glanced at Mother. Her face was shining like that of an angel.

My father was not as distressed by my conversion as my mother. In fact, at a Passion play which we attended in Union City, New Jersey, with three friends of mine, sometime before my entrance to the monastery, he identified the five of us with the disciples of Jesus. He would not show such a sympathy before my mother in deference to her strong Jewish feelings—he well knew that, had he done so, she would have felt completely isolated and crushed. It was bad enough having a son who was a Catholic! I noticed the reverence in his demeanor, a reverence which came over him when we entered St. Patrick's Cathedral to attend Mass at which Archbishop (then Msgr.) Fulton Sheen was preaching.

I had the opportunity to visit Mother at my sister's home in Cleveland, where she lived the last few years before entering a nursing home at the recommendation of her doctor. I also visited her at the nursing home—a Catholic one, Mount St. Joseph, in Euclid—which has beautiful grounds, which no doubt attracted her and my sister to it. The Sisters of St. Joseph and St. Mark, who have a genuine love and respect for the elderly and infirm, took very good care of her, and she loved them in return. After two and a half years there, Mother died January 3, 1978, at the age of ninety-five. She remained a good Jewess and, I believe, very close to God.

Epilogue

Herbert Schwartz entered the Church and was the founder of Mount Hope, a large Catholic community of single and married people in Middletown, New York. He died a few years ago. Bill Gorman was a valued discussant at the Center for Democratic Institutions in Santa Barbara, California, headed by Robert Maynard Hutchins. He co-authored a book with Mortimer Adler, *The American Testament*, and also worked with Mortimer Adler on the Encyclopedia Brittanica, and other projects, such as "The Hundred Great Ideas." He died of cancer in Santa Barbara, where he lived with his wife.

After learning that Bill had cancer, I visited him when I was in California conducting a series of dialogues for our Trappist monks at Vina. After this, Bill made a retreat at St. Joseph's Abbey on two occasions, urged to do so by his Jewish wife, who wished him to take advantage of all the opportunities which his religion could afford him. Herbert Ratner also entered the Church. From 1937 to 1940 he was a senior member of the Committee on the Liberal Arts at the University of Chicago. He was in general practice and was associate clinical professor of Family and Community Medicine at Loyola Medical School in Chicago, and the Commissioner of Health of Oak Park, a suburb of Chicago. He is the editor of *Child and Family*, a quarterly magazine, and the only American consultant on the Pope's Commission for the Family. He is a noted and much sought-after international lecturer.

Robert Maynard Hutchins played an important role in the development of St. John's College in Annapolis, Maryland, whose curriculum features the Great Books, and in the promotion of the Great Books for adult education. Dr. Adler's career is too spectacular to require mention. Author of many books, some of them best-sellers, like *How to Read a Book*, and Chairman of the Board of Editors of the Encyclopedia Brittanica, he heads the Institute for Philosophic Research in Chicago, and continues to do important work.

I write this fifty years after my entrance into the Church, forty-six years after entering this Trappist Cisterican Community, and thirty-nine years after ordination to the priesthood. My love for Jesus and His Body the Church has grown and grown by His grace. He has made me increasingly aware of the tender love that His Father and ours has for all His children, the whole human family, and the great designs He has for it, if it will accept them. I realize that Jesus' greatest work, for which He redeemed the human race and sends His Holy Spirit to sanctify it, is to reveal to us His Father. Thus, in Jesus, we become sons of the Father and have eternal life.

The Jewish people know God as their father, but they do not know God the Father in the fullest sense. A father or mother is only father or mother because they have a child or children. But the Father's children are not only human beings: He is before all a father through having a Divine Son, who became man. In acknowledging His Son, we know the Father more truly and more deeply. Jesus, by His redemption and by revealing to them the Father, made all human persons the Father's children.

In the Divine Mind, we are all one in Christ, sharing by grace His divine sonship. This is why the Father loves us so tenderly and dearly. He wishes to be a part of our life and to make us a part of His life, all of us whomsoever we are.

This is what I have come to realize more deeply in these fifty years; this is the object of my contemplative monastic vocation. It is to this that, in loving Jesus and the Father, I respond with my whole mind, heart, and strength. It is about this, and the increase of mental health that follows from it, that I have written in my book on the spiritual life, *Hammer and Fire*, published in revised form by St. Bede's Publications.

To assist me in being fully responsive to the Father and to Jesus, I count on the example and intercession of Mary, the Mother of God and of men and women, who most fully entered into the mind of her Son, Jesus. She shared His life, His devotion to His Father, and His desire that all come to know and love this Father, Whom Jesus alone can reveal, and Whom she herself reflects by her love, kindness, compassion, and gentleness. She, being overshadowed by the Holy Spirit, became His bride, that Jesus and all of us without exception, might be her children.

Notes

[1] *Physics*, chapter 8; *Metaphysics*, chapter 10.

[2] This can be seen in Mortimer J. Adler's most recent book, *Ten Philosophical Mistakes. Basic Errors in Modern Thought—How They Came About, Their Consequences, and How to Avoid Them*, (Macmillan, 1985).

The Truth Shall Set You Free

The Truth Shall Set You Free

Ronda Chervin

(Ronda Chervin, the editor of this volume, is Professor of Philosophy at St. John's Seminary Theologate in Camarillo, California, and the wife of Martin Chervin, also a convert. She is the author of many books including The Church of Love; The Way and the Truth and the Life; Christian Ethics and Your Everyday Life; *the* Prayer and Your Everyday Life *series; co-author with Sister Mary Neill of* The Woman's Tale; Bringing the Mother with You; *and, with Don Briel, of* How Shall We Find the Father? *She lectures internationally.)*

*　　　*　　　*

Shout joyfully to God, all you on earth, sing praise to the glory of His name. . . . Hear now, all you who fear God, while I declare what He has done for me (Ps 66:1-2, 16).

My story has a somewhat unique beginning—nothing! As children we learned *nothing* about God. God was as real to us as Zeus is to you. Although there was a long line of rabbis on the Sephardic Jewish side of the family, and my paternal grandmother was a very devout Protestant, so totally had both my parents rejected religion that it was never discussed except in the fashion with which one might refer to the views of some remote tribe of primitive men.

My twin sister and I took it for granted that our school friends who went to Jewish or Catholic services were going solely because they were forced to by their superstitious or tradition-bound parents. In fact, not a single one of our friends ever talked about religion to us in a believing manner. We had never seen the inside of a synagogue or a church, and when our Protestant grandmother, who was heartbroken at our atheism, once tried to teach us some simple prayers, we mocked her and made fun of the verses. She died long before our conversion, but now I often picture her rejoicing in eternity as she watches her grandchildren at Mass, adoring the same Christ whom she alone in the family worshiped for so many years.

My father has since told me that once my sister and I asked him to take us into the neighborhood Catholic church and that we sat spellbound through two Masses. Actually, I do not remember the incident at all. Mostly, as children, we associated Catholicism with the fear inspired in us by the Catholic near-delinquents on our street in the middle of New York City.

Once, a band of older boys encircled us on our way home and demanded to know what our religion was. Their purpose was to decide what epithets to throw at us and whether to beat us up or not. When they had exhausted every religion they knew of and we still replied in terrified negation, they asked us directly what we were. Since they had never heard the word "atheist," they let us go. Not a highly edifying example of Catholic spirituality, yet one which remained lodged in our minds for years to come.

I do not think I was an especially reflective child. Still, I remember writing a composition in high school which demonstrates the early beginnings of a philosophical search for meaning. We were asked to write about what we wanted to be when we grew up. I wrote that I did not see how one could choose what one wanted to be until one could discover what the meaning of life was. Surely these two questions should be connected, although in fact for most people they rarely are. But this was just a passing thought, and by the time I entered college I had forgotten about it altogether and was bent only on finding some occupation which would be interesting and exciting.

Not in vain philosophy

While a freshman at City College of New York, the problem of meaning surfaced again. No matter what subject I studied, I was dissatisfied because we never got to the really important questions. If it was a course in government, we discussed different forms of rule, but we never explained why there should be government at all. If the subject was psychology, we would learn about how people behaved, but never about what a man ought to be or why he existed in the first place. Finally, I came upon a field which questioned everything: philosophy. I decided to major in this fascinating subject which I had never heard of before.

The way in which philosophy was taught at nonreligious schools in the 1950s and 1960s was rather skeptical and destructive. Reasoning was not expected so much to help one arrive at truth as it was considered a tool for critique of any view that dared to propose itself as truth. The student was to read an article by any philosopher and score points by refuting as much of it as he could. Although I thoroughly enjoyed becoming expert in critical methods, I could not help but feel disappointed. Was there no philosophy which was invulnerable to attack? No philosopher who had a truth which could withstand even the thrusts of my agile brain?

I remember one day becoming deeply upset and begging my favorite teacher to tell me how I was to go about living if, in fact, there was no truth. My skeptical professor answered in a very interesting way. He said that I was asking of philosophy what only religion could give. That was all he said.

I never found out whether this professor had a religion. The reason? In those days it was considered the gravest sin of academic life for a professor to try to influence the student to accept his own views about philosophy and even more about God. Therefore, the religious beliefs of the professors were entirely hidden from us. Although Christ said, "I am the way, the truth, and the life," teachers who were followers of Christ would give courses about truth and life and never mention the name of Christ.

Nowadays, sophisticated professors in Catholic schools are beginning to adopt this same neutralism in class. I regret this profoundly, because I know that I was not alone among my fellow students in being lost and confused. Our greatest unspoken wish was to find a teacher who could help us find a saving truth. The thought that many of my teachers at college actually believed in Christ yet thought it unprofessional to mention it, still leaves me with a feeling of bafflement and sorrow. Perhaps with their help I might have been spared the three years of despair which preceded my introduction to Catholic thought.

During my college years, in spite of a growing doubt as to whether philosophy had any ultimate meaning, I continued to study it for lack of a substitute. In the meantime, I proceeded to seek an emotional meaning for life, but my friendships could not fill the void within. This was partly because I had no sense of what a human being was or how he ought to be treated or where strength could be found for fidelity in love. I had not the slightest interest in the separate identities and problems of my boy friends, nor did I feel in any way responsible toward them.

Ethical viewpoints were as nonexistent to me as religious ones. The question of right or wrong did not enter my head, and I thought that people at college who worried about such matters were narrow-minded and even psychologically abnormal. I could not understand at all why so many of my fellow students at the University of Rochester, to which I transferred for my junior and senior years, were so engrossed in questions about God. The fact that they discussed such matters by the hour only confirmed me in my feeling of superiority. A person who does not have any answers to the questions of life usually does not face the true despair which lies behind his or her fierce pleasure-seeking activities and arrogant poses. Now I realize that the ethical and religious people at college were wiser than I, if not so clever, and more sensitive to the good, if not as psychologically and aesthetically aware as I was.

Kierkegaard, the Danish philosopher and theologian (in his *Sickness unto Death*), stresses the fact that most despair is hidden behind poses of strength. Finally, these masks are torn away and the anguish which had always been there is revealed in its true frightfulness. This happened to me only when I entered graduate school at Johns Hopkins in Maryland.

I was still studying philosophy out of lack of anything better to do. I already had come to despair about human relationships, so I did not wish to live with the other students in the graduate dormitory. A fanciful dream floated around in my head about finding truth in the solitude of my own being by starting again from scratch to read each philosopher in isolation. And so I chose an apartment far from campus for my solitary research. I had begun to read existentialist books, and, although I did not understand them very well, I grasped the mood of alienation which permeates so many of these writings. When I read the works of the religious existentialists, I could not grasp their theistic solutions to the dilemmas of our time because faith was to me remote and still unreal.

As it turned out, living alone was just what was needed to force me into crisis. I became lonelier and lonelier. Philosophy at Hopkins was even more skeptical and depressing than at the other schools I had attended. One dreary evening the abyss which no love or truth had been found to fill opened itself and swallowed me up. I found myself hysterically suicidal. Terrified of my own emotions, I rushed out of my apartment in the night to join my friends in the once scorned graduate-student dormitory.

At one time, the idea of young people even contemplating suicide was considered to be extremely unusual. Now, unfortunately, suicide has become one of the chief causes of death among the young. Many present-day thinkers find causes of the growth in suicide rates similar to those at work in my life—an absence of genuine love, loss of ethical standards, and a frightening void in the place previously filled by God.

Seek out the lost sheep of the house of Israel

But suicide was not to be my fate, for new characters now entered the scene—personalities which I had never even dreamed could exist: wonderful, good, intelligent, *Catholic* people. Here is how it happened. By one of those coincidences which believers call providence, my mother turned on a TV program called the "Catholic Hour," because the speakers were philosophers and she thought that would interest me. The program was an interview with Dr. Dietrich Von Hildebrand of Fordham University and Dr. Alice Jourdain (later to become Mrs. Von Hildebrand) who had a great apostolate among Jewish students at Hunter College.

These two people impressed me, so I decided to write them a personal letter—something I had never done before to any stranger. I wrote to Dr. Jourdain about my philosophical despair. It turned out that she lived only two blocks away from my home in New York, and after an hour's talk with her I knew I was facing the greatest turning point of my life. Never had I met a person like Dr. Jourdain. While she spoke to me of her love of truth, she looked directly into my eyes with an expression of love and concern such as I had never seen in the face of another human being. My meetings with her opened up an absolutely new world of values—mysterious and unknown to me but so powerfully attractive that they filled me with a new, unbelievable hope and joy. At the risk of losing my fellowship at Hopkins, I left Baltimore after just half a year and enrolled at Fordham University in New York City to seek truth anew in a Catholic milieu.

It is very hard to explain the impression that a Catholic university, in former times, would make on an atheist. All those stained-glass windows in Gothic-style library buildings and chapels, those images of Christ on the Cross in the classrooms, and those gentle statues of the Virgin Mary—all taken for granted by Catholics—affect the atheist with bewilderment, wonder and, sometimes, enchantment. They bespeak a source of beauty older and richer than that produced on the contemporary scene, a source of truth beyond the functionalistic computer theories of knowledge, and a source of love beyond sexual and emotional attraction.

The unique spiritual atmosphere of Fordham intrigued me, but a person with a philosophical bent rarely becomes a convert to Catholicism solely through admiration of architecture, music, incense, ceremony, or even appreciation of the solidity of tradition. For a lover of wisdom, it is usually impossible to convert without first seeking with one's mind to determine the truth of religious beliefs. For this reason the often-asked question, "Did you convert for emotional or intellectual reasons?" is misplaced. The genuine conversion of a philosophical person will almost always include both elements. The intellect must bow to a truth acknowledged to be rightly superior to it, because it descends from the mind of God. But also the emotions must consent joyfully to what has been revealed; otherwise the truth would lie solely in the intellect without the power to transform the personality from a lifestyle of disbelief to a living faith. The process of my conversion to Catholicism, which will be described in what follows, involved the continual intermingling of intellect and heart, truth and love.

What attracted me primarily to the professors at Fordham University's Graduate School of Philosophy was that combination of truth and love which visibly animated them; this was in startling contrast to what I had experienced of teachers in other schools. These had a deep love of truth, and they believed in the truth of love. That these attitudes flowed naturally from belief in a true God of love was not understandable to me, yet I was filled with excitement because of it, and I would arrive home in the evening after classes overflowing with ideas to discuss with my amazed family. How could so much enthusiasm come from contact with such a dead medieval superstition as Catholicism?

Preambles to Faith

It is not possible to relate in detail the unfolding of those philosophical notions which began to convince me that there was, indeed, truth in Catholic philosophy. However, it may be interesting to summarize these thoughts because they include truths which are no longer as clear to many Catholics as they used to be.

You will recall that when I entered Fordham, my views about ethics and the nature of man were totally skeptical. It took my professors no time at all to refute ideas which were considered to be incontrovertible in the contemporary philosophy I had previously studied. For example, the skeptical point of view toward truth holds that there is absolutely no way for man to attain any certainty about any important facts or opinions. Nothing is true for all, there is only "truth for me." By a refutation as old as Augustine in the fourth century, my professors at Fordham could show that skepticism was itself contradictory. Some truths must be held to be objective. "Even if I err, at least I know that I who exist err," stated St. Augustine.

Von Hildebrand, who was my professor in theory of knowledge, showed that when the skeptic claims "there is no truth," he is at least making a truth-claim for that very statement. That there is no truth is supposed to be really true and not just his own opinion. Hence, the statement is self-contradictory, since if it is true, there is one truth; and if it is false, there is also a truth. To a reader untrained in philosophy, such arguments may seem trivial indeed. For those who have racked their brains about such questions for years, such arguments are crucial; for without belief that truth can be found, the whole enterprise of thought is undermined.[1]

With respect to ethics, the typical nonreligious university was, and still is, dominated by the theory of relativism. Relativism holds that all our views of right and wrong are mere products of conditioning forces of a historical, social, biological, or psychological nature. When a man says, "This is morally wrong," he is only revealing the results of his conditioning. To study the subject of ethics as if one could find out what is good and evil in itself on an objective basis is rendered ridiculous if relativism is true. Is it not foolish to make great pronouncements about what is absolutely good and evil if one cannot even transcend one's culture, if one is trapped by suppositions rooted in one's own background?

To this contemporary viewpoint, Von Hildebrand was totally opposed. According to his philosophy, the fact that people in different cultures may have different moral ideas does not change the fact that there are some basic moral truths which are either universal or should be so.[2] Every society values justice. Every man knows the difference between kindness and malice; between fidelity and betrayal. Every man has an idea of a moral "ought" which transcends his own immediate desires. Even the man who claims that morality has no absolute validity—because he holds that ethics can be reduced to conditioning—in his own daily life will respond with moral indignation to the breach of those rights which he personally holds to be inalienable. The same man who defends relativism when he is teaching as a professor will become enraged if he sees some minority being ill-treated. Shall we say that his disgust with injustice is foolish, since he does not believe that there is such a thing as justice? Rather we should suppose, Von Hildebrand argues, that in his life he rightly affirms objective ethical norms which he finds hard to analyze philosophically. He should change his philosophy to conform to his intuitions.

But if there are objective moral norms, how can one explain the diversity in the ethics of people in different cultures? This is explained by Von Hildebrand in his book, *Ethics*, with the concept of "value blindness." A man who justified slavery in the South of the United States, for example, did so because he was blind to the fact that people he enslaved were human beings with the same rights as whites. Because his society condoned this practice, he did not realize the gravity of his act. Some individuals were able to overcome this blindness. They had insight into the human dignity of every man, and they succeeded in awakening others to the inherent value of the enslaved people.

The concept of value blindness not only explains diversity but also makes way for the hope of real moral progress. No matter how blind a person may become to a moral truth—and even if he should convince the majority of people in his country of his false viewpoint—he cannot destroy the absolute value of a human being. The moral law transcends his thoughts and judges him. If all men are equal in essential humanity, then this truth transcends and judges any individual or society which would deny men such rights.

What was especially intriguing to me about the theory of value blindness was that, from the point of view of my professors, I was to be judged a victim of it, because values which were evident to them were unknown to me. Foremost among them were the values of purity and humility.³ This discrepancy between the virtues held dear by the people I had come to admire most in the world and my own views caused me to turn my critical acumen against myself for the first time in my life. I began to get an inkling of what was meant by Kierkegaard's view that there is a sort of Copernican revolution in the soul of a man when he comes to see that it is not he who judges existence, but existence which judges him.

That summer after my first semester at Fordham found me in this state of mind. I could see that there was a truth worth seeking, and I knew that moral values were real and objective, not merely conditioned and subjective. I vaguely thought that materialism could not be correct if there were such things as nonphysical truth and moral norms which were higher than society. But I could not see at all that these concepts had anything to do with the existence of God. Still, it was clear to me that my professors had qualities which I had never seen among humanists. There was a loving quality in them which I had never found elsewhere in such purity and intensity; they claimed that all this goodness emanated not from themselves but from God.

Beauty is Truth, Truth Beauty

Then I had the good fortune to go on a Catholic Art Tour of Europe run by one of my philosophy professors, Dr. Balduin V. Schwarz (later to become my godfather). I had never appreciated architecture or painting before, but under the tutelage of Professor Schwarz I came to be overwhelmed by the greatness of Church art. When our tour group entered the Cathedral of Notre Dame in Paris, I burst into tears, overwhelmed by the beauty and spiritual intensity of that wonderful church.

Through this encounter with religious art, I came to experience a new aspect of man: the spiritual dimension. Some new depth was being awakened in me different from what I had experienced in the intellectual and emotional spheres.

It was not long before I wanted to know what the people believed who had built these magnificent churches. I must express my gratitude to Professor Schwarz who spent almost all his time on the bus rides between sights patiently answering the hundreds of questions I came up with. He gave me a little New Testament to read. I had never read the Bible. I read the story of Christ with fresh eyes and became thrilled by his personality.

Most converts from atheism first come to believe in God and then try to decide whether or not the Person Jesus was God. For me the process was reversed. In the Person of Christ depicted in the Bible, I sensed for the first time what the divine is. I came to see what Professor Schwarz meant in marveling at the *uninventibility* of Christ. To claim that later Christians just made up the figure of Christ as a ruse to start a new religion, as some skeptics claim, was unthinkable: they would have had to be holy themselves to invent such a personality, and if they were holy, they would not have lied.

The sense of the divinity of Christ, which came through reading the Gospels, was heightened by a religious experience. When our tour came to Rome, we went to the Vatican Museum. We stopped for only a few seconds in front of a tapestry by Raphael depicting the miracle in which Christ tells Peter and the other apostles to let down their nets after they had failed all night to catch any fish. There is a luminous smile on the face of Christ as he lovingly watches the apostles bending over their overflowing nets. As I looked at the tapestry, I felt the divinity of Christ flowing through his humanity, just as if he had been standing in person before me. So intensely did this picture strike me that an inner conviction of the divinity of Christ overcame all doubts which still lingered after reading the Gospels.

During the same few days that our tour spent in Rome, I had another great experience. Our group was to have an audience with Pope Pius XII. I had thought before the trip that this part of the itinerary I could easily skip, but Professor Schwarz insisted that I go. He was so anxious for me to see the face of the Pope that he brought a little footstool for me to stand on.

The sight of the Pope's face was one of the most unforgettable moments of my life. I was touched by the total and luminous humility of this man whom I had pictured as a haughty, pompous relic from former times. I saw his overflowing love as he beheld a poor stricken child who had been brought to be blessed. The humble love in his demeanor as he looked at the suffering child made a deep impression on me. I felt then that truly such a man could not be nourished by falsehood and hypocrisy and that the Catholic Church might be holy after all.

When I came back to the university after our tour, I continued to study Catholic philosophy, but my greatest interest was in reading books of apologetics. Writers such as C. S. Lewis, Chesterton, and Newman were able to show in an intellectual manner why it was rational to accept what is beyond reason: the mysteries of Christianity. For example, C. S. Lewis in *Mere Christianity* shows that it is impossible to conceive of Jesus as a mere man, or even the best of men, because a man who claims to be divine is either crazy or really authentic.

The books of Newman, especially his *Apologia* and his *Development of Christian Doctrine*, show why the need for unity of religious truth depends upon one Church guided in matters of doctrine by the Holy Spirit. My own way of explaining this comes out of years of studying philosophy. Christ comes with a message of love. In order to spend our time loving, we cannot be expending all our energies in theological debate. Faith in dogma gives us a source of truths we can be certain of so that we can go ahead and worship and love instead of bickering or setting up rival sects.

The Leap of Faith

Yet something was still lacking. I longed to be a Catholic, but I did not think I had enough faith to take the step. The moment of total conviction was a strange one. I had been praying that I might have the grace to believe in such a way that I could fully commit myself to Christ. I had been told that I must leap into the arms of Christ and that this would require a moment of courage. I feared desperately that I would not be able to make this leap and everything would be lost.

Then it seemed that Christ himself took my hand and led me across the gulf between doubt and total faith. After a session with a priest for formal instructions in the Catholic faith, I was walking down the street and suddenly I believed totally and simply and happily.

I then lived in anticipation of Baptism, which was on January 4, 1959. My godparents were Professor Schwarz and his wife Leni, whose love and kindness and patience with me then, and still today, are indescribable. The devil had his last inning by appearing at the Baptism in the form of a cockroach in the baptismal font, but I was too frightened of making a mistake in the ceremony to scream, as I would have done ordinarily. After the ceremony I burst into a flood of tears, not of remorse but of gratitude for Christ's loving salvation.

The time after Baptism was the hardest. I had imagined that with entrance into the Church would come immediate sanctity. I thought that all time would stop. Then came the slow-moving drama of daily Catholic life which is shared by born Catholics as well as converts. It is a question of holding fast to all the moments of grace in the midst of humdrum times. Daily, one must remember that life is to be lived toward God; that Christ is present at every moment waiting for us in the needs of people. One must turn toward him in every mood, to accept his love and be refreshed and created anew. There is always the memory of the central miracle of conversion: that Christ found me forlorn and helpless in the confusion of the ways of the world and drew me by his love into his fellowship and the friendship of Christians.

I can truly say that through the years the faith I have in the Church has grown rather than diminished. I have never had a moment of serious doubt. Every year the doctrines of the Church seem to me to be more deep, clear, and beautiful.

Great moments of coming deeper into the mystery have included coming to see that Christ is love, just as much as he is truth, and experiencing that love in a personal way. Meeting the Holy Spirit in charismatic prayer led to tremendous joy and sense of God's living presence within.[4] More recently, consecration to the Immaculate Heart of Mary has brought a flood of contemplative graces.

The reader may be wondering what my atheistic family thought of all this religious activity. At first they were quite bewildered, but then began a period of intense argumentation, followed by genuine interest on their parts. A few years after my own Baptism, my twin sister Carla came into the Church. She has since become a pioneer in liturgical dance. Some years after my sister, my mother also became a Catholic. I shall never forget the tears of joy my sister and I shed on the occasion of the Baptism of our mother. How amazing that our prayers had helped give spiritual birth to the one who had given us our physical birth.

My husband, brought up in an orthodox Jewish home, became an atheist in his youth, then a "fellow-traveller" of the Catholic Church for years, and was baptized six years ago.

My father, the author of atheistic tracts, keeps up a running dialogue on religion with me, and I hope that the prayers of my readers will be added to mine for a miracle for him also.

In rereading my own story, I am overwhelmed by the graces of God, by his great love for me, a child of darkness. With his truth he set me free. May he, by his love, bring me safely Home.

Notes

[1] For a more detailed discussion of the problem of truth see: Von Hildebrand, *What is Philosophy?* (Milwaukee, 1960).

[2] Von Hildebrand, *Ethics* (Chicago, 1972). This book contains his detailed work on ethical theory. A shorter book by Von Hildebrand, *Morality and Situation Ethics* (Chicago), contains an excellent refutation of the "new morality."

[3] Von Hildebrand, *In Defense of Purity* (Chicago, 1970).

[4] See *Why I am a Catholic Charismatic* by Ronda Chervin (Ligouri, MO: Ligouri Publications, 1976).

Is Anybody There?...Does Anybody Care?

Ross Frankel

Is Anybody There?. . . Does Anybody Care?

Ross Frankel

(Born in 1962, Ross Frankel, the youngest of our converts, has been a student at Loyola Marymount University, is employed as an accountant, and is planning to study theology in preparation for the ministry.)

*   *   *

Every now and then the words "Is anybody there? Does anybody care?" still fill my mind. But there once was a time when I whispered the phrase nightly, for over five years. No longer do I despair of such abandonment—it is as if a century has passed since then, with so much occurring, and yet I still recall clearly how the problems were overcome, the steppingstones traversed.

To give you an idea of what I am like as a person, I enjoy almost every aspect of life because I find God's presence within all things. From woodworking and automobile care to baking pies and washing windows, from driving to work to the pressures of accounting, I find a hidden pleasure; often the most tedious, boring tasks for others are for me a gateway to refreshing change and renewed growth of life. Life for me now is lived simply, one day at a time, and not overly preoccupied with any one thing. God is my focal point in life (though, I admit, it may not always seem to be the case), with the universe being a guide to Him.

All this despite my determined and stubborn character, my formerly skeptical heart, my heritage and upbringing. In a family where philosophers, psychologists, and science post-graduates are the norm, the prevailing views are a skeptical, if not cynical, approach to a man-centered world. Religion has had little place in a world where man seems to think that the direction of the future is solely up to him.

Family Background

Where did this former attitude come from? In part, from my

father's people: Jewish (Sephardic) immigrants who watched as a world, and presumably a God, turned their backs on saving whole populations from extermination. And from my mother's people— German, Scottish, and a multitude of other nationalities—who also watched as their neighbors, upstanding members of various church communities, showed how little they understood their beliefs. To understand these backgrounds is partially to understand the influence upon my life, and upon my decision to follow the Father, Jesus Christ, and the Holy Spirit.

"Grandma," my mother's mother, has touched my life more than any other member of our family. Not of Judaic background, yet much of her seems more authentically Jewish than some of my father's family members. Her wisdom (eighty years and still vibrant), reaches out to me whenever we get together.

To my grandmother, her relationship with "this superior being some call God," is a personal, private, one-on-one dialogue of prayer. For many years I didn't know this of her, for she abhors those who wish to push their beliefs on others. Thus, she has no wish to do so, either. She also attends no single church regularly, as she does not want to feel locked into any one set of ideas, but is interested in what everyone has to say.

From Grandma, I have learned to listen to all sides, to keep an open mind, but also to question and not blindly accept anything.

From my parents, I received a strong dose of skepticism. Even though Momma has come to believe in a superior being, for much of her life she lived with twentieth century humanistic secularism. With degrees in engineering and psychology in an era when mankind generally believed that it could accomplish anything—and was doing so—without God's help, Momma developed little interest in devoting her time and energy to serving something that probably did not exist or at least was not interested in the plight of humanity.

Further, because she is an ardent supporter of traditional family life, she is very skeptical when she hears that a family member has become a church member. She feels that he or she may toss aside the family for God, as a passage in the Bible seems to suggest. Thus cults and organized religion, especially Catholicism which has religious orders which seem to replace the family unit, are suspect to her. She is very concerned that she may lose her family to such.

On the other hand, Momma has been carefully and slowly growing interested in Judeo-Christian thought. In her work as a psychologist, she has come to find that a person who has a healthy religious belief also is mentally healthy, while those with psychological problems most often hold unhealthy religious beliefs. She hopes to learn why this correlation exists.

The skepticism of Grandma and Momma is joined by the more cynical view of humanity of my father. As with my mother, Dad's outlook has been influenced by his scientific background. Dad does do the best he can to live a good life, but he doesn't seem to have a place in his life for a relationship with God and doubts He exists.

Further, Dad, who has seen so much corruption in religious and other organizations, rejects organized religion in almost any form as being merely the business of lazy and conniving shysters out to syphon off money, energy, and time from the able-bodied but ignorant person.

These three people—Grandma, Momma, and Dad—have made the greatest impression upon me. And despite my new religious beliefs, I still have a skeptical streak, though I try to be open-minded.

An Introduction to God

My first years of school were at a public school, where God was not spoken of. But in second grade I transferred to a Lutheran school. There I quickly realized that I was different from everyone: classmates and teachers were all deeply involved in the church's community, with a reverence and awe of some being called "God." The families of classmates, too, seemed devoted to this God, while my family kept to itself. I felt out of place.

I knew nothing of God—nor did I really want to know, at first. In the beginning I thought "God" was just another game to play. And yet as time passed, it seemed that these people really believed in what they called the "Three in One." Even a couple Jewish classmates said they knew God; I seemed to be the only one who didn't believe.

Although to my teachers and classmates I must have seemed very indifferent about God, I *was* curious and asked my grandmother about the things I heard in school. Grandma explained to me many concepts that one would not expect a second-grader to understand, but God had blessed me with a good and inquisitive mind, and I was able to comprehend, to a degree, all she told me of biblical translations and the resultant problems, figurative and poetical language, and so on. I also had been taught a little German and Spanish, and this helped reinforce my understanding of translation problems. Grandma helped me to see that when the Bible said a town was destroyed by fire and brimstone, it could actually mean that a volcanic eruption had occurred. So, at that time in my life, I enjoyed imagining different possibilities for the interpretation of the Bible stories.

But the classroom situation didn't allow for personal discussion, and I never mentioned the things I discussed with my grandmother to anyone. So outwardly I must have seemed indifferent in my attitude toward God and religion.

Because of this apparent indifference and my lack of participation in church, a young pastor called me into his office one day near the end of the school year—just to talk, I was relieved to hear. He asked me if I believed in God: Father, Son, and Spirit. My answer, that I didn't know and wasn't sure, in its honest way, seemed to surprise him. I think he had expected me to say that I simply didn't care. He also asked me if I believed that the Bible was God's Word, to which I replied, remembering my grandmother's comments, that I didn't think it could be word for word accurate after two thousand years, having probable translation errors. I also said that I thought the stories in the Bible were kind of nice, but that I didn't see what they had to do with my life. At that point, I remember him saying to me that I had a better grasp of what was going on than most of the other students!

Because I was at last able to speak one-to-one with someone about religion, the subject from that moment became a point of interest in my life, and the question of who or what God was began to grow within me. In fact, learning about God became exciting, but, I should point out, purely as a matter of curiosity, not spiritually. I let my imagination take off—thinking then that there might be such things as ghosts and spirits.

Unfortunately, these one-on-one talks were not to continue: the young pastor was called away to another school, and my grandmother did not live close by, so I wasn't able to see her as often as I would have liked. But at least it was a beginning for me.

About this time I began to meet some of my father's relatives. One, an uncle, was a devout member of the Jewish faith, a cantor. I recall being told that I, as a Jew, was one of God's chosen children, different and apart from others by my very nature. I guess that this feeling of being apart from everyone became a reason in itself for my then becoming somewhat withdrawn. I struggled with the feeling that to be different was wrong, yet heard more and more that my Jewish heritage made me different.

Anyhow, being of Judaic heritage, but with no particular Judaic beliefs, made me feel out of place with my Jewish relatives. And, by the time I entered junior high school, I also felt out of place in my immediate family because I seemed to be the only person with even a slight interest in religion.

I had very few friends in junior high—partly due to my belief that I was an outcast of sorts. The few friends I did have ended up either moving away or proving not to be true friends in one way or another. Not wishing to be further mistreated or hurt by new friends, I slowly withdrew from my peers—and even my family—becoming a loner.

During this time I delved into the world of science fiction and fantasy, such as Tolkien and books on ghosts and witches. *Star Trek* and a horror show on television were my daily entertainment. The escape to such worlds and the search for *something* became more pronounced. I realized that something was lacking in my life, that I had to find it, and if I could figure out what *it* was, then I would be happy again.

After a while, I realized that science fiction showed few signs of hope. The void within me, which felt like a dry lifeless desert, was growing; it desperately needed to be filled with some sort of life. I felt as though I was going through hell—hell to me being a complete absence of love, a lack of someone being there whom I could love and who could love me. Is anybody there? Does anybody care? Those words rang out in my mind, hoping that if God existed, He would hear and answer. Maybe He didn't exist. Maybe He did—but I had to know *now*.

For short periods of time I could forget this interior battle by becoming a workaholic. I tried many things: swimming, yard work, culinary arts, scholastic study, partying (when did I sleep?). Anything was better than trying to deal with the inner desert that swept over me when I was not occupied. Anything was preferable to the sheer pain of loneliness. Anything was better than waiting for an answer from a mute God.

As my later teen years passed, I no longer seemed to be comfortable anywhere. Grandma, the one person I did feel comfortable with, had so many problems of her own, I had little desire to add mine. I kept everything pent up inside. I felt utterly useless, incapable of pleasing parents, teachers, or peers. My one hope was that someday in the future something would change. That feeble hope was all that kept me going.

Awakening

Deciding that for practical reasons the nearest university, Loyola Marymount, was tolerable as a college for me—since my sister came through without converting from atheism to being "one of those wretched Catholic nuts"—I figured the religious atmosphere would not bother me. Not knowing what I wanted to major in, I decided to get the required liberal arts courses out of the way. One class, the Philosophy of Man, was being taught by a former professor of my sister. Sounded reasonable.

Enter Dr. Ronda Chervin into my life. Simply just another professor to me much of the time, she introduced me to a concept which was to turn my life around and spark in me the beginnings of a genuine belief in God.

Pascal's "Wager," basically, is that, if there is no God and no Hell, yet you believe that there is, and so you try to live your life in a God-centered and ethical manner, you lose nothing except bad habits and ways. And if there is a God and you try to live as best you can according to His will, then you will gain everything—so what is wrong with that? Either way, you lose nothing and gain much by believing in God.

Thus, I privately decided to bet on God. I was still a little skeptical as to His existence, and only considered my personal gain in my alliance with God. Yet, it wasn't long before God, who now had a foot in the door of my life, let me know that He did indeed exist. This strange experience dramatically reinforced my tentative commitment to a solid, permanent one.

One summer day, while standing at the top of a ladder, I was warily pruning a tree-fern. The ladder stood near the edge of a three-foot wall which surrounded a dirt embankment, and just above a driveway filled with sharp-edged machinery and car parts. The day was very calm; there was no wind.

Without warning, the ladder collapsed, sending me and it towards the driveway, a drop of ten to twelve feet. I could see that I would land on my back, amid spiked pieces of metal—serious injury was certain.

And then suddenly something struck my back, pushing me towards the embankment of soft earth, leaving the ladder to continue its plummet onto the machinery. As it seemed that a human hand had saved me, I turned around to thank whoever it was—but there was no one to be seen anywhere on the entire street!

One might think I was hallucinating or that it was a branch that had struck me. But no, there was no branch or anything of the sort in the area, and I could still feel the sting of the slap on my back—that much I knew to be real.

I entered the house, took off my shirt, looked into the mirror and saw a large red mark on my back—the distinct impression of a human hand with less clear but still definable outlines of fingers. All I could think was that there was no physical evidence whatsoever of anything that could have made such a mark, from this material world. It was therefore, I felt, most likely to be proof of a spiritual world's existence and its active role in affecting the material world. I had at last found evidence of a spiritual world.

My conclusion was that, if some force had executed a kind act, then, the mere possibility—let alone the probability—of a force of good at work would indicate there could also be a malignant force as well. Thus, a seemingly outlandish idea of a Supreme Good battling a Great Evil—God vs. Satan—now became a probability. The existence of hell also became conceivable.

At that point, and for a couple years, I pledged my allegiance to God mainly because I now suddenly feared hell. This may not have been good theology, but at least I was taking another step in the right direction. With my distrust of organized institutions, I hesitated about joining any religious groups, but after some time, I came to consider that my Judaic heritage should be fulfilled by my becoming a member of Judaism; after all, it seemed to me the least offensive, least authoritarian, most intellectual, and most festive. And so I quietly prepared, for over a year, to make my Bar Mitzvah (though I never did).

Growth and Conversion

Despite this religious conversion, by my junior year in college I had become almost completely a hermit in terms of social life. I had further sworn off any close friendships due to having had so many turn sour. My desire was simply to work and study. Yet, as orientation week began, I was called to be a guide for the new transfer students. Among the group were three individuals who, despite my efforts to remain aloof, found their way into my heart as friends. Josie and Barbara helped me to learn that Catholics were really ordinary people, and not the crazy nuts I feared (even though I was attending an open-minded Loyola, I was still suspicious).

The other, Dave, a loner like myself, gradually spent more and more time with me, becoming almost a member of my family. Inch by inch he mentioned Jesus in passing, but without forcing his ideology upon me. And gradually I came to accept that Jesus wasn't the nut I had made Him out to be either, but rather the big brother and kindly master I had never known.

Dave, who had for half a dozen years been a Protestant Pentecostal (one whose life is living in and using the gifts of the Spirit), brought me to—of all places—a Catholic Church's young adult group, where I soon joined him as a member. I was still wary and suspicious of the Catholic Church, yet, as I read Vatican II documents, I came to realize that the Church had some merit after all.

Debating the question for several weeks, I finally said to God, "I have come to the point in my life where I find a need to be part of a community of people who love you. I just ask that you show me which denomination of Judeo-Christianity would be best for me." I didn't expect an answer. My answer, or the one that seemed to come to me, was the Catholic Church. (Note: don't ask unless you are really prepared for God to answer you.)

"You cannot be serious," I begged of God, "but if this is what is best, then I will accept. However, I must understand the following concepts..." whereupon I listed troublesome points about the Catholic faith, everything from the Eucharist to Mary.

Four days later, while studying the sixth chapter of Mark's Gospel for a theology class, suddenly information, tons of information, all in regard to the Eucharist filled my mind. It was as though everything I had heard in my classroom studies and in prayer groups suddenly came together, but now in a logical and reasoned order. "The Eucharist makes sense!" I cried. My father, in the same room, muttered that it was time to take me to a psychologist. Personally, I wasn't sure if that would have been a bad idea; after all, God doesn't speak to just *anybody* does He?

Within the next six months, saints, the priesthood, and several other points of doubt were resolved in similar fashion. I now felt ready to become a member of the Catholic Church.

It is usual for a person interested in joining the Church to go through two years of study and inquiry. I never knew this, so I simply decided to spend my summer vacation studying Catholicism, conversing with some clergy on a weekly basis.

It was during one of these sessions with a spiritual director that another difficult problem was resolved for me with the help of God. It concerned the position of Mary in God's Kingdom.

I had come to the point where, if I could not find a way in which I could accept Mary's position in Catholic doctrine, which I saw as anti-scriptural and idolatrous, then I could not truthfully take my baptismal and confirmation vows.

So here I was, debating for hours with my spiritual director and seeing no hope in sight. I was praying desperately to God for a solution when the telephone suddenly rang, and my director left the room to answer it.

While he was gone, I continued to pray, trying to regain control of my strained temper and asking for spiritual guidance. And then, in a most extraordinary way, it seemed as if I heard the voice of God Himself, explaining to me the role of Mary as our spiritual mother. This and all my other misunderstandings about her were quietly and prayerfully cleared up, and, by the time the experience was over—it all happened in about five minutes—I was able, from my heart, to accept Mary as my own spiritual mother.

Baptism

But my instructions did not proceed well: because of scheduling problems, no single advisor was able to remain with me for any length of time. The resulting lack of continuity caused me to become frustrated, and I wondered if God really wanted me as a Catholic Jew after all. With anger in my voice, I told Him off. I stipulated that if He really wanted me, He had better help me so that I could be baptized and confirmed on my twenty-first birthday, no less.

At this point, Dr. Ronda Chervin re-entered my life. One day I told her of my troubles in studying, that I wanted so much to celebrate my coming into adulthood by beginning a new life as a member of the Catholic Church. She handed me a catechism book—some six hundred pages—and asked me to read it and be ready to answer ten to twelve *hard* questions. Two or three weeks later, I passed her test with flying colors, whereupon I was recommended for baptism and confirmation.

On the evening of my birthday, at a parish near Loyola, a professor/priest officiated at my entry into Catholicism. The day had been a tense one with an examination in one of my classes, friendships crumbling (again), family feuds, and so on. I didn't see how the celebration could possibly be carried off. I just didn't know what to expect next.

When the water of baptism was poured over my head and the chrism was placed upon my forehead, I finally—for the first time in my life it seemed—felt a deep sense of quiet, a sense of peace I had never known before, a sense of blissful silence.

With a smile on my face, and few words, I walked out of the church with the small gathering of family and friends and my godmother, Ronda, preparing to have a celebration dinner with everyone. As we looked into the beautiful sunset we found a prismatic vapor trail had formed from a missile test, and it seemed to be a bird, a dove flying downwards towards us. . . .

* * *

As I think back on these events—three years since my baptism—I find the whole experience to be very dream-like. I see how God took my by the hand, and I know I'll never again feel completely deserted; people may come and go, but He will remain. Now, as I am considering studying for the priesthood, I can sense His presence. I see myself as Jewish *and* Christian, and I plan to grow in both heritages.

I see myself also as very fortunate, for I have found a caring Father; a Friend, Brother, and Teacher in Jesus; and a Companion and Counselor in the Holy Spirit. I know now that Someone *is* there, and Someone *does* care.